The Victor
KNOW&
BELIEVE
Series

Bob Smith

This book is part of The Victor KNOW & BELIEVE Series, an eight-volume library of the major doctrines of the Bible all of which are written in a clear, down-to-earth style. Other books in the series are:

The Bible: Breathed from God (Bibliology), Robert L. Saucy, Th.D.

The Church: God's People (Ecclesiology), Bruce L. Shelley, Ph.D.

The Future Explored (Eschatology), Timothy P. Weber, Ph.D.

The Holy Spirit: Comforter, Teacher, Guide (Pneumatology), Fred P. Thompson, S.T.D.

The Living God (Theology), Robert D. Culver, Th.D.

Jesus Christ: The God-Man (Christology), Bruce A. Demarest, Ph.D.

Man: Ruined and Restored (Anthropology), Leslie B. Flynn, B.D., M.A.

Salvation: God's Amazing Plan (Soteriology), Millard J. Erickson, Ph.D.

Editor of the Series is Bruce L. Shelley, Ph.D., professor of Church History, Conservative Baptist Theological Seminary, Denver, Colorado.

VICTOR Know and Believe SERIES

The Living God

Robert Culver

Edited by Bruce L. Shelley, Ph.D.

While this book is designed for the reader's personal enjoyment and profit, it is also intended for group study. A leader's guide is available from your local Christian bookstore or from the publisher at $2.25.

VICTOR BOOKS

 a division of SP Publications, Inc., Wheaton, Illinois
Offices also in Fullerton, California • Whitby, Ontario, Canada • London, England

Dewey Decimal Classification: 231.1
    Subject headings: THEOLOGY, GOD

Library of Congress Catalog Card Number: 78-53576
ISBN: 0-88207-765-1

VICTOR BOOKS
A division of SP Publications, Inc.
P.O. Box 1825 • Wheaton, Ill. 60187

Contents

Foreword

Signs of evangelical vitality are all around us. Prominent personalities from politics, sports and entertainment have recently "come out" for Christ. Publication houses report record sales of evangelical titles. Large conventions of evangelical believers catch the eye of the national wire services and the major magazines. The public is discovering the meaning of "born again."

This rather sudden exposure in the secular press has a happy side and a sad side. The happy side is the opportunity for millions of Americans to encounter the Gospel of Jesus Christ. For a half-century biblical Christianity has received mostly scorn from the spokesmen of American culture—movies, newspapers, novels and television. The public was so busy laughing at the Gospel that it couldn't listen to it. Today, some are listening.

The sad side of this exposure is the evident weakness of "born again" religion. The major polls reveal that it is largely experience-centered, and almost any weird brush with mystery seems to do.

Biblical Christianity has an experiential element, but it is linked with doctrine and Body. It is what we think and to what we belong as well as what we experience.

That is where this book and others in the Victor KNOW & BELIEVE Series come in. These eight books, designed for personal or group studies, aim at adding truth to testimony. As evangelicals, we should not only speak up in American society; may we say something when we do.

Bruce L. Shelley
Editor

7

1

Talk about God

"Thou art the Lord God" (1 Kings 18:37).

The most striking statement in the whole Bible may be the first one: "In the beginning God created the heaven and the earth" (Gen. 1:1). The Bible begins with talk about God. It also ends that way (Rev. 22:19-21).

There is no preliminary introduction to the leading Person or idea. From the start, God is simply there. Scripture seems to assume that the man who hears the Bible read for the first time already has the idea, in his world of thought, of a Person called God. God's name appears 28 times in the first chapter of Genesis—God did this or God said that—yet not a single sentence is devoted to identifying Him. It says nothing about where God came from or what He is like. Later in Scripture, God is contrasted with other gods who are regarded by some as real. Unlike them, He is "the Maker of heaven and earth." But there are few formal statements about His "essence and attributes." The position of the authors of Scripture seems to be that men come to the Bible knowing that God exists. The purpose of Scripture is to provide information about God and lead men to an acquaintance with the One who is their Creator.

This spirit and outlook were shared by the Reformation fathers who shaped the great creeds and confessions of the sixteenth and seventeenth centuries. Luther's *Shorter Catechism*, for the instruction of the children of believing parents, begins: "I believe that God has created me." John Calvin, who after 400 years still informs most evangelical Protestant teachers, began his great *Institutes of the Christian Religion* with the sentence: "Nearly all the wisdom we possess, that is to say, true and sound wisdom, consists of two parts: the knowledge of God and of ourselves."

Most informed students of the Bible are convinced that men do not need to be told that God exists. Men already know too painfully well that He does. The Christian mission is often to clear up the garbled understandings of God with correct information and to relieve the conscience of its weight of guilt, provided, of course, that the Good News is received into the heart. To bring men true knowledge of the living God can cast them into the dust of despair. Like the Israelites before God's presence at Sinai (Deut. 5:23-27; Ex. 19:16-20; Deut. 18:16) and that startled man in the Gospel (Luke 5:8), they are apt to cry "Depart from me . . . for I am a sinful man." Or like Isaiah, they may exclaim, "Woe is me . . . because I am a man of sinful lips and I dwell in the midst of a people of unclean lips" (Isa. 6:5).

General Awareness of God

But let us press the point further. Basic to all the preaching and exhortation of Scripture is the assumption that men already know something about God. They are not unaware of their dependence on Him or their accountability to Him. The Book of Jonah furnishes a striking example. The Hebrew prophet, after obstinate delays, finally did preach his divinely imparted message in the great, pagan city of Nineveh. He cried, "Yet forty days, and Nineveh shall be overthrown" (Jonah 3:4). "So the people of Nineveh believed God, and proclaimed a fast" (3:5).

When the word came to the king of Nineveh he joined in, announcing national repentance. "Let them turn every one from his evil way. . . . Who can tell if God will turn and repent . . . that we perish not?" (3:8-9) The pagan Ninevites evidently had a greater realization of divine truth as a ground for evangelism than did the scripturally informed Jews of Jesus' time. For the Lord said, "The men of Nineveh shall rise up in the judgment with this generation, and shall condemn it: for they repented at the preaching of Jonas; and behold, a greater than Jonas is here" (Luke 11:32).

This knowledge of God which sinful men have brings them neither pleasure nor peace, for the knowledge they have is largely guilty knowledge. The prophets of Old Testament times relied on this guilty knowledge, even in heathen hearts, to rebuke their sins. Amos, for example, directed prophecies of judgment against five of the neighbor lands of Judah and Israel (Amos 1:1—2:6). God condemned Damascus for excessive violence in conduct of war (1:3), the Philistines for unnecessary cruelty (1:6), Tyre for treaty-breaking (1:9), Edom for lack of fraternal feeling and murderous anger (1:11), Ammon for atrocities against the women of a conquered district (1:13), Moab for desecration of a neighbor people's cemetery (2:1).

On the other hand, even without the support of supernatural revelation, mankind has been helped by this knowledge of God. It has improved morality and restrained evil. Almost all of the world's best art has reflected the Creator. Families seem to be moved by a dim awareness of the dignity and beauty of the home. Parents seek training for their children and improvement of their lives.

The Bible goes on to show that the "Creator of heaven and earth" is not some obscure principle or power. He is a special Being who tolerates no rivals. Though many claim deity, there is but one Being in the category of *God*. In the first chapter of the Bible, His name is God (Hebrew, *Elohim*). This designation is joined with Lord, (Hebrew, *Jehovah*) in the second chapter. Several other names and namelike terms appear later. But they all belong to Him who is true deity, "The Lord (*Jehovah*) our God (*Elohim*) is one Lord" (Deut. 6:4).

Necessity and Importance of Worship of God

Following the narrative of creation and the fall, Genesis provides a report of the earliest efforts of men to worship God. That is the primary importance of the story of Cain and Abel (Gen. 4:1-15).

Its relevance to doctrine is immediately apparent. No discussion of God's being, person, or attributes precedes the story. We simply learn that the first two men born into the fallen race were fully aware that God is, and that if God exists He may not be ignored, as we have come to ignore background music. If God the Creator exists (and we know He does) then man, the only rational creature on earth, must worship Him as the angels in heaven do. The two sons of Eve knew this. We do not know how they came to have this information. But know it they did. And all generations of men since have known no less.

God Alone Is God

There are several biblical reports of public contests in which some spokesman for the Lord demonstrated to men that the God of Israel, and He alone, is God.

Let us consider one rather famous example we read about in 1 Kings 17—18. In a time of national apostasy, Elijah the Tishbite suddenly appeared before King Ahab announcing the beginning of a contest between Jehovah and His prophet, on the one hand, and the fertility gods and goddesses of the Canaanite pantheon with their many so-called prophets on the other.

The significance of this conflict appears near the end of Elijah's prayer and in the people's response: "Elijah the prophet came near, and said, 'Lord God of Abraham, Isaac, and of Israel, let it be known this day that Thou art God in Israel, and that I am Thy servant, and that I have done all these things at Thy word . . . that this people may know that Thou art the Lord God' " (1 Kings 18:36-37). Immediately, the fire of God fell on the water-soaked sacrifice which Elijah had prepared and consumed it, together with the stones of the altar and the wood. Then, "when all the people saw it, they fell on their faces, and said, 'The Lord, He is the God' [*Jehovah* is the *Elohim*]" (1 Kings 18:39).

This is not the only such contest reported in the Bible but it is certainly the most striking one. Such episodes are in the Scriptures to teach us. What do they teach? That God has demonstrated that He is true by the mighty acts of power performed at His messengers' word. In each case, the messengers of God were authenticated by the same great acts of God's power. Other such incidents are reported in 1 Kings 22 and notably in Jeremiah 28 (see also Psalm 106).

This doctrine that God alone is God is nowhere spelled out more faithfully than by Paul in his first letter to the Corinthians. The common knowledge that God the mighty Maker does exist was important to the Greeks. But the truth had been perverted. Public religion in Greece was a gross, expensive, corrupting worship of many gods. At Corinth there was a particularly offensive feature of Greek culture. Idol worship got mixed up with the marketing of meat. It was hard to buy meat in the "shambles" (butcher shop, 1 Cor. 10:25) that had not been previously offered in worship to an idol.

What should a Christian do? Believers there wanted to know. So Paul wrote, "As concerning, therefore, the eating of those things that are offered in sacrifice unto idols, we know that an idol is nothing in the world, and that there is none other God but one. For though there be that are called gods, whether in heaven or in earth (as there be gods many, and lords many,) but to us there is but one God, the Father, of whom are all things, and we in Him; and one Lord Jesus Christ, by whom are all things, and we by Him" (1 Cor. 8:4-6). In view of the nonentity of gods other than the true God, Paul went on to say, the flesh of animals offered to an idol by someone else had not been affected. So meat could be bought in the market and eaten in all good conscience by a Christian (1 Cor. 10:25).

The Names of God
One does not read far in the Old Testament until he learns that personal names are important. The first human name, *Adam,* is the Hebrew word for "ground, soil, or earth," signifying that man's body is taken from natural elements in the soil. *Eve (Ava)* means "life," signifying that Adam's wife is mother of all who live. *Cain* means "smith" (metal worker), indicating the origin of metallurgy among his progeny. *David* means "beloved," *Solomon,*

"peace" and so on. Each indicates something that hopefully will be in the character or history of the person designated.

The same is true of the biblical names of God. When we speak or write about God and when we address Him, we must employ some name or namelike term. *God, Elohim,* and *Jehovah* have already appeared in the pages of this book. Surely we should be acquainted with His own self-designated names. In each case, these reveal an important characteristic of God. Several of God's names arose out of believers' experiences with Him. They supply marvelous insights into God's ways with men as well as aspects of His holy character.

Space does not allow us to consider all of these names. They are all compound, such as Jehovah-*Jireh* (the Lord will provide) and Jehovah-*Isidkenu* (the Lord our righteousness). But let us look at the most frequently used and most significant ones.

The Song of Moses—A Mine of Information

Near the end of his life, Moses, the great lawgiver, delivered a series of sermons to his people, the children of Israel. Transjordan had been conquered. They were poised to invade Canaan under fresh leadership. Before taking leave to die and go home to God, Moses composed a song which he recited before the assembled tribes. It is recorded in Deuteronomy 32:1-43. Most of the common biblical names of God appear in the first fifteen verses.

YHWH (Deut. 32:3, 6, 9, 12, 19, 27, 30, 36, KJV, usually rendered *Lord*). "For I proclaim the name of Jehovah" (Deut. 32: 3, NASB). This is the personal, proper name Israel had for their God. Later in the song, Moses said, "For Jehovah shall judge His people" (v. 36), showing again the special character of the name as personal. The word *judge* here means mainly "to rule as a magistrate." After the exile, Jews came to revere the name, Jehovah, so much that they thought it wrong even to pronounce it. Many feared that if it was spoken at all, it might be "vain" and doom the speaker to hell (see Ex. 20:7). So the pronunciation was lost. Most modern scholars feel that *Yahweh* was the ancient pronunciation.

Ancient Hebrew was spelled without vowels. Medieval Jewish scholars supplied the vowels of *Adonai* (Lord), with some modification, and in reading aloud pronounced Adonai, as today. When these vowels are read with YHWH an approximation of Jehovah comes out. This word, now firmly in the idiom, is not likely to be displaced in common speech.

When God explained the meaning of this name to Israel, He emphasized its connection with: (1) God's *promises* and *presence*. God said He would be with Moses and His people, Israel (2) God's *salvation* (deliverance). The Israelites were to be rescued from the bondage in Egypt. (3) God's *provision* for their every need (see Ex. 3:1-22; 6:1-8).

It is not surprising, then, that when Moses got around to writing the first books of our Bible, he used the name *YHWH* most frequently when he reported God's saving work on behalf of His people. The name enters the Christian tradition through the Hebrew name *Jehoshua* (Greek, "Jesus"), which means, "Jehovah saves" (see Matt. 1:21).

Elohim (Elo-heem) (Deut. 32:3, 15, 17). "Ascribe ye greatness unto our *God*" (Deut. 32:3). From the biblical point of view, "This name properly represented One only Being, who revealed Himself to man as Creator, Ruler, and Lord. It was His own peculiar title, and ought to have been confined to Him" (R. B. Girdlestone, *Synonyms of the Old Testament*, Eerdmans, 1948, p. 19).

We do not know what language was spoken in Eden, but *Elohim,* or its equivalent in that language, is represented as the proper designation of the Creator. It is the only one used in the first chapter of Genesis. "In after ages the worship of the Creator as Elohim began to be corrupted. The name, indeed, was retained, but the nature of Him who bore it was well-nigh forgotten. When men were divided into different nations, and spoke various dialects and languages, they must have carried with them those notions of Elohim which they had inherited from their fathers, but the worship which was due to Him alone was in the lapse of ages transferred to the souls of the departed, to the sun, moon, and stars, and even to idols made by men's hands" (Girdlestone, *Synonyms,* p. 20).

So we read of "strange" *elohim* (Gen. 35:1-4). When Rachel ran off with her father Laban's images he demanded his *elohim* back (Gen. 31:19, 30). Jacob, who did not regard them as genuine deities, nevertheless, for purposes of communication, used Laban's word (verse 32).

Elohim is God's title, meaning deity. *Jehovah* is His personal name. In keeping with this, people in Scripture said, "my Elohim," but never "my Jehovah." He is "the Elohim of Israel," but never "the Jehovah of Israel."

In Moses' song in Deuteronomy, there is an example of the use of this word *elohim* as a "courtesy title" for heathen deities [nondeities] while reserving the title for the God of heaven and earth whose name is Jehovah:

> "And He [Jehovah] will say, Where are their gods [elohim],
> The rock in which they sought refuge . . . ?
> Let them rise up and help you
> Let them be your hiding place.
> See now that I, I am He,
> And there is no god [elohim] besides Me:
> It is I who put to death and give life.
> I have wounded, and it is I who heal;
> And there is no one who can deliver from My hand"
>
> (Deut. 32:37-39, NASB).

Hatsur (The Rock) (Deut. 32:4, 15, 18, 30, 31). "The Rock, His work is perfect" (v. 4). *Rock* is a transparent figure employed as a name of God and means cliff or bedrock such as we might find at a quarry site (see Isa. 51:1). Throughout this song of Moses, it stands for God's great stability and is in apposition with Jehovah, Elohim, and El (vv. 3-4, 17-19, 30-31). He is the only sound foundation for the life of a man or a nation.

As the Rock He is the source of salvation for sinful man, "the Rock of his salvation" (v. 15). David prayed to the Rock:

> Let the words of my mouth,
> And the meditation of my heart,

Be acceptable in Thy sight,
O Lord, my Rock and my Redeemer
(Ps. 19:14)

This name is specially connected with our Lord in His pre-incarnate life. Referring to the wilderness journeys of Israel, Paul wrote: "our fathers . . . did all eat the same spiritual meat; and did all drink the same spiritual drink: for they drank of that spiritual Rock that followed them: and that Rock was Christ" (1 Cor. 10:1, 3-4).

Paul was affirming not the *typical* presence of Christ, but His *real* presence with Old Testament believers, as He is with us to-day. There is only one Mediator of salvation: "For other foundation can no man lay than that is laid, which is Jesus Christ" (1 Cor. 3:11).

O safe to the Rock that is higher than I,
My soul in its conflicts and sorrows would fly;
So sinful, so weary, Thine, Thine would I be;
Thou blest Rock of Ages, I'm hiding in Thee.
(William O. Cushing)

'El (The Mighty One) (Deut. 32:4, 18, 21). "A God ['el] of truth and without iniquity, just and right is He" (v. 4). This name usually designates the true God. It likely derives from a verb meaning to be strong, to be in front of, hence the term, "the mighty One."

Unlike the similar word, *Elohim,* this name is often joined with *Elyon,* another name of God. So we read of "the most high God" (Gen. 14:18), "the Almighty God" (*El Shaddai,* Gen. 17:1), "the God of Beth-el" (*El Beth-El,* Gen. 31:13), and "the God of thy father" (Gen. 49:25).

In Exodus 34:6-7, 'El is used with a whole constellation of names for God and namelike adjectives: "Jehovah, the Lord God ('el, a mighty One) compassionate and gracious, slow to anger, and abounding in lovingkindness and truth; who keeps loving-kindness for thousands, who forgives iniquity, transgression and sin; yet He will by no means leave the guilty unpunished, visiting the iniquity of fathers on the children and on the grandchildren to the third and fourth generations" (NASB). This statement is without parallel in Scripture.

Father (Deut. 32:6). "Is not He thy Father that bought thee?" Moses is referring to the fact that their God, like a father who begets a child, had brought them into existence as a people. Of the standard English versions only the NASB capitalizes Father here. The idea of God as Father is strongly supported, however, by the prophets (Isa. 64:8, and Mal. 2:10) and by Jesus. Opening verses of 19 of the Epistles of the New Testament refer trustingly to God in this way.

'Elyon (The Most High) (Deut. 32:8).

When the Most High gave the nations their inheritance,

When He separated the sons of man,

He set the boundaries of the peoples

According to the number of the sons of Israel (NASB).

This verse means that God as Most High has apportioned each nation, throughout history, their lands, just as He did Israel.

The name *'Elyon* occurs most frequently in connection with God's rule over the affairs of nations (Dan. 3:26; 4:17, 24, 25, 32, 34; 5:18, 21; 7:25) and in the expressions of divine worship in the Psalms (Ps. 7:17; 91:1, 9).

The name *Elyon* is formed from *'alah,* which means "to ascend." Thus the name suggests that God is the ascended, the highest (being). It is an idea of God which people who have never heard of the God of Scripture readily accept. What is that *something beyond* all created beings? *Elyon.*

There are two other important names of God found in the Bible which do not appear in Deuteronomy 32. They are *Shaddai* and *Adonai.*

Shaddai (Almighty). The word is plural in form—usually held to be a plural of majesty. "I am *Almighty* God, walk before Me, and be thou perfect" (Gen. 17:1).

This title indicates the fulness and richness of God's grace. It reminded the Hebrew reader in a graphic way that we have not because we ask not, and that every good gift comes from God.

Properly understood, *Shaddai* is an exceedingly graphic term.

There is a Hebrew word for a mother's breasts, *shad,* usually (and understandably) dual, a pair (see Song 8:1; Hosea 2:2; 9:14). This word seems to be the source of *Shaddai.* For example, in the last appearance of the word in Genesis (Gen. 49:25), Jacob blessed Joseph and said, "From the *El* of thy father, there shall be help to thee; and with *Shaddai,* there shall be blessings to thee, blessings of heaven above . . . blessings of the breasts [*shadayim,* the two breasts] and blessings of the womb."

Adonai (Lord). This is a special plural form of the normal word of respectful address to another male, especially a superior— Master, Lord, Sir. Used of God, it means the same thing except that being a plural, like *Shaddai,* the aspect of respect is heightened.

The term reminds us that God is a great King. We may come boldly to His throne of grace (Heb. 4:16). Yet we must at the same time "offer to God an acceptable service with reverence and awe: for our God is a consuming fire" (Heb. 12:28-29, NASB).

Theological Significance of Names

The biblical names of the supreme Being tell us much about who He is, what He is like, and what He has done, as well as what He now does and shall yet do. "Taking the Books as they stand, the important point to notice is that the various names are used by the sacred writers advisedly, so as to bring out the various aspects of His character and dealings" (Girdlestone, *Synonyms,* p. 38).

The terms give color and power to the many promises and warnings involving God's names. "They that know Thy name will put their trust in Thee" (Ps. 9:10).

Come, Thou Almighty King,
Help us Thy name to sing,
Help us to praise;
Father, all glorious,
O'er all victorious,
Come and reign over us,
Ancient of Days.

2

Reasons for Believing in God

"The heavens declare the Glory of God" (Ps. 19:1).

A short time ago, on a return flight from the Holy Land I sat in an aisle seat, and my wife in the seat to my left. Members of our tour group frequently passed questions to me or stepped down the aisle to talk. I frequently spoke about God in my answers and other conversation.

Near the end of our journey at Kennedy Airport an angry looking little man across the aisle first made a very disparaging remark about my voice and then sarcastically asked, "What gives you the idea that the Person [God] you keep referring to even exists?"

I first made a courteous acknowledgement of his presence, and then replied, "I have been explaining just that to about 500 students in a series of 30 lectures. Do you want the whole course or just a summary?"

Already regretting his antagonistic sally he mumbled, "Just the summary."

So I gave him a 20-minute summary. But I felt utterly right in starting off with this confession in answer to his first question: "I believe in God because, like all people before they invent reasons for disbelieving, I find it much more intelligent to believe than not to believe."

The man was badly shaken, but I am certain the statement is

correct. I remain convinced it was the right thing to say to that man at that moment.

Belief, believing, and their synonyms are used in this chapter to mean "simple acknowledgement of the existence of something," but this is only a small part of the full Christian meaning.

In sermons and lectures I sometimes try to clarify the difference by asking: "Will everyone here who believes in a personal devil please raise his hand."

When almost everyone else has his hand up I say, "Put your hands down now. *I* do not believe in the devil. I believe in the living God."

The effect is sometimes more devastating than I desire, so I've quit doing this. But the point is, we may accept something as a fact which we may wish were not a fact. Our language permits me to say in such a case, "I believe in a personal devil."

Belief in God Is Universal

In exactly this sense, men everywhere do believe in God. This is not to say that their ideas about God correspond to biblical teaching about "the God and Father of our Lord Jesus Christ," or that their ideas about Him are well defined. Yet, as we saw in chapter 1, the idea is sufficiently definite that several Scripture writers do refer to the fact that the Gentiles (heathen, nations)—people without direct knowledge of the biblical revelation—are aware of God's existence. Paul, for example, spoke of the Athenians ignorantly worshiping God (Acts 17:22-28).

Not all men *seem* to believe in God. This, in part, is because of our ability to put unwelcome knowledge out of our conscious thoughts. Just as some people put their illnesses or serious problems aside as if they did not exist, living in a fool's paradise, so men glorify Him not as God (Rom. 1:21) and their Creator is not even in their thinking.

Others affirm belief in God but are dissatisfied with Him. They suppose they know more of justice, morality, goodness, beauty, and truth than He. They weary the Lord with their words (Mal. 2:17) —sometimes long treatises on philosophical themes.

A few participate in religious forms but, in their hearts, they live without Him. "The fool hath said in his heart, there is no God" (Ps. 14:1). This fool is not a dogmatic atheist but a practical atheist. He may be a church elder or the village priest, but he is a hypocrite, for "in his heart" life goes on as if God did not exist.

Why Do Men Believe in God?

Why do men universally "believe" in God? Some excellent theories have been proposed as to why this *consensus gentium* prevails. Some have argued that this common belief is a remnant of primitive truth. By this, they mean truth known in the early generations of the race when God had daily connection and dealings with men, as Genesis 2 and 3 report. Supposedly, this truth has been passed on in garbled form through all generations to the present.

There may be something to this, but it appears likely that some sections of the race would have failed to pass the knowledge on. It seems more in harmony with the Bible to find the source on a deeper level.

Others have suggested that the common belief in God is based on inferences from the observable phenomena of nature. Maybe all of us make this inference, but if so, there seem to be no parallels. Inductively acquired notions are seldom universally held.

A Spontaneous Development? George Park Fisher, an American Presbyterian theologian of a century ago, said the conviction that God exists arises in quite another way, " . . . belief in God is not in processes of argument. His presence is more immediately manifest. There is a native [that is, born-in] belief, arising spontaneously in connection with the feeling of dependence and the phenomena of conscience, however, obscure, undeveloped or perverted that faith may be" (*Grounds of Theistic and Christian Belief,* Scribners, 1902, p. 24). In other words, God made each man—the first man and all his descendants—with a potential knowledge of God. When we come to full awareness of the external world and of our inner thoughts, an awareness of God appears.

The awareness is dim and only partly formed in some, for many of us are neither very reflective nor especially alert to ideas. In others, the awareness of God is clear and well formed.

God a First Truth? Since very ancient times, at least as early as the Greek philosophers of the fourth century B.C., many learned men have said that God is immediately present in men's minds as one of several *first truths*.

A. H. Strong, author of the most enduring and widely read book of Baptist theology, puts this universal awareness of God in the category of *first truths*. By this pregnant expression, writers mean truths existing in the mind previous to thought or reflection. They are truths the mind unconsciously presupposes in order to think about any subject whatsoever.

Sometimes, these *first truths* are called *innate ideas,* ideas we are born with. Such ideas are not held to be consciously present at birth or even when first used. Yet when experience through the senses furnishes data for the mind to reflect on and shape into concepts, the mind is already furnished with categories which arrange and file them.

Thus, when we perceive the distance between A and B, the idea of *space* or *distance* immediately moves from *latent* existence to *patent* existence in the mind. A man employs the idea of space without ever being taught it or experiencing it. Similarly, when something happens within an infant's little world, such as a loud noise, he looks for a *cause*. Cause is another first truth, innate, not produced by experience.

Now, according to this approach, God is one of these first truths. The *latent* idea springs up in the mind at a certain point in every man's conscious life. It may be at the first awareness of wrongdoing, or the first interest in cause-effect relationships.

Correspondence of Two Worlds? We may defend this view of things by a slightly different approach. There is an external world (sea and land, clouds and sky, men and things) to be observed. I observe it; you observe it; almost everyone does. We each enter into knowing relationship with it, for we find, so to speak, mental shelves, bags, hooks, slots and drawers which help us arrange these numerous bits of information. Colors, we might say, go in certain shaped bags, distances on shelves, values in drawers, pleasures in slots, and pains on hooks.

So, my inner mental world, in a general way, *corresponds* genuinely with the external world. When I talk with you I discover that you respond in similar ways. We both *know* the external world and can actually have discourse about it. How? And why? Because Someone greater than all observable reality has put all reality in these relationships. I must assume Him in order even to think about *me, you,* or *it.*

You may say simply that the external world which we see, feel, touch, hear, and taste corresponds with our inner world which knows the outer one. Why? God makes them to correspond.

Conscience the source? As G. P. Fisher suggested, conscience may be a source of the universal notion of God. Conscience, Paul wrote, either accuses or excuses us (Rom. 2:15). It must exist in us all because all men make moral judgments.

If we do conclude that all men have this moral sense, then this God, whom our consciences fear, must be exceedingly great in wisdom and power. Whether He is also gracious or not is a question conscience does not answer, for conscience gives the soul of man small comfort. The sinner receives assurance of forgiveness following repentance and confession all right, but not from conscience. It comes from the revealed Word of God (See Ps. 32:1-5 and compare 2 Sam. 12:1-13; see also 1 John 1:8-9).

If we hold the view that conscience helps explain the universal awareness of God, then we have every reason to make the same assumption the Bible makes: men do not need to be introduced to the idea of God. They all know about Him.

The Bible does assume that men believe in the existence of God and that men's ideas about Him are sufficiently correct to make conversation about Him possible. We must accept this if we are going to address men's minds as Paul did at Athens (Acts 17:16-34). Once we accept this universal awareness as a fact, we

have the privilege and duty of initiating Christian witness to anyone on earth on the basis of it.

Why Men Should Believe in God

Why should men believe in God? It is a fact that sizeable numbers
of men have rejected their "belief" in God. They "hold [suppress]
the truth in unrighteousness . . . Because that when they knew
God, they glorified Him not as God, neither were thankful; but
became vain in their imaginations, and their foolish heart was
darkened. Professing themselves to be wise, they became fools"
(Rom. 1:18, 21-22). Scripture holds these folk responsible for
denying and perverting their knowledge. Yet, they are not only
to be loved as God loves them (John 3:16; Rom. 5:8) but also
to be hated as God hates them (Ps. 139:21; 97:10).

What shall we do when we meet the wholly secular mind? We,
of course, shall declare the Gospel. If a man will not consent to
hear it, then if we can get his attention, we may try some arguments to get him to consider his ways. This also is to declare the
Word of God, for some of these arguments are part of Scripture
too. As we do so—if we have done our homework—we will find
our own Christian faith strengthened while we raise questions in
the minds of our listeners about their smug practical atheism.

Some years ago, a practicing Christian psychologist addressed
the students and faculty of Wheaton College on the question of
whether or not psychology can be used to convert unbelievers to
Christ. He said, in sum, "No, not as such. Many people are not
fully sane and some are not sane at all. The Gospel is addressed
to man's rational understanding. He will therefore remain a lost
man until some degree of sanity is restored. Otherwise he cannot
even hear the Gospel. If psychological counseling or psychiatric
treatment can return him to sanity, then the Gospel's power can
operate in him and he may be saved."

In a similar way, if a "professing-himself-to-be-wise" man, who
has rejected native belief in God, will stand still long enough to
hear some arguments for God's existence, one or two things may
happen to him. First, he may open his mind just a little to the idea

that God exists. The moment he does so, his conscience will produce shame for his guilty unbelief. Second, while he listens to my arguments, I shall also be declaring some of my own faith and reporting some of God's Word. That man therefore is "dangerously" close to being under Gospel power.

Now, what are those arguments for God's existence?

The Causal Argument

The argument from the present existence of the universe is also called the Argument from the Idea of First Cause or the Cosmological Argument. It begins with the fact of the universe and asks the question, How did it get here? Then it answers, The universe was created by an adequate cause. The name given to this Adequate or First Cause is God.

Unless one is willing to affirm, as certain people do, that the universe is self-caused and eternal, one must admit that the "heavens and the earth" began at some point. Strong puts the argument this way: "Everything begun, whether substance or phenomenon, owes its existence to some producing cause. The universe at least so far as its present form is concerned, is a thing begun, and owes its existence to a cause which is equal to its production. This cause must be indefinitely great" (A.H. Strong, *Systematic Theology*, Judson, 1907, p. 73).

Objections have been raised to this argument. Some want to know if instead of *first* cause where "the buck stops," perhaps an infinite regress of causes may be just as logical. According to a Hindu myth, the world rests on the back of a great elephant, the elephant's feet rest on the back of a gigantic turtle. Sometimes the turtle is said to be swimming in a great sea. Ask the Hindu what contains the great sea and all he can do is shrug his shoulders or change the subject. Is this just as reasonable and believable as the argument for First Cause?

Others wonder if we must find the cause of the heavens and the earth outside the universe. Must the cause come before all else and be outside the universe? Perhaps the cause is the same age as the universe (coeval) and immanent, that is, dwelling within the world. If so, then make the universe itself the cause and you have Pantheism. All that exists is God and His infinite expressions. This is the philosophy underlying several oriental religions. And it is currently in vogue in America, in Rosacrucianism, Theosophy, and Transcendental Meditation.

Another objection takes the shape of a frontal attack. An aged professor challenged my faith in college days by sarcastically asserting: "I can as justifiably posit an eternally existing, self-sustaining universe as you can an eternal, all wise, all powerful Creator-God." But a world such as that must run by eternal, immutable laws and forces.

What shall we say? In the first place, an infinite regress of causes is generally unsatisfying to thoughtful people. It is a solution undesirable for almost any problem we can think of. The mind seeks a *resting* place. Furthermore, there is clear evidence of a master design through all the parts of the universe. There must have been a beginning at some point when the design was made by an intelligent being. The idea of infinite regression is a very weak explanation. It is really to give up making any explanation. The same objections prevail against both pantheism and the notion of an eternal, uncaused universe.

Furthermore, the evidence of observation both casual, unlearned observation and technical, scientific research clearly indicates that the universe is neither self-sustained nor eternal. It had a beginining.

Poetically stated, we observe to our distress:
Swift to its close ebbs out life's little day.
Earth's joys grow dim, its glories fade away.
Change and decay in all around I see.

Everything we see is temporary and dependent on something else. This includes that portion of our own beings we know to be part of the natural order, our physical bodies. Scientists who search the skies with instruments and research have established that our universe is moving toward infinite dissipation at a regular rate.

Analysis of light from the stars with an instrument called a spectroscope shows that, like painted dots on the surface of a toy balloon being blown up, each spot in the universe is moving farther from every other spot. Names given this phenomenon are Red Shift, Doppler Effect, and expanding universe. The farther the objects in space are from one another the faster they accelerate toward infinite velocity. Though evidence has been sought for a slowdown at the borders of the universe, none has yet been established. The universe could not have been operating in such a way from eternity past or else it would now be infinitely dispersed.

Another fact of common observation, formalized by science, is that the world's available energy is running out. The world is running down. There will be as much matter and energy at the end of time as now, but energy will be locked up in ways prohibiting its use. When the sun has dissipated all its matter and energy to the extremities of the solar system our world will be at an end. The law of entropy (namely of unavailable energy) will have had its say. What if the sun had started giving off its energy an eternity ago? Then the solar system would have disappeared, along with our earth, long ago.

The Bible, moreover, contains several extended sections on the created heavens and earth. These constitute a message about God to His rational creatures everywhere. It was not a philosopher, but a sensitive shepherd boy grown up, who wrote: "The heavens are telling of the glory of God; and the firmament is declaring the work of His hands. Day to day pours forth speech, and night to night reveals knowledge. There is no speech, nor are there words; their voice is not heard. Their line has gone out through all the earth, and their utterances to the end of the world. In them He has placed a tent for the sun, which is as a bridegroom coming out of his chamber; it rejoices as a strong man to run his course. Its rising is from one end of the heavens, and its circuit to the other end of them; and there is nothing hid from its heat" (Ps. 19:1-6, NASB).

Several matters are clear in this passage. God has placed a message about Himself in the created heavens of the sun, moon, and stars. There, His majesty and power may be seen (v. 1). The message is 'round the clock (v. 2) and is a silent testimony (v. 3), peculiarly susceptible therefore of being ignored. The messengers are beautiful and vigorous (v. 5) and they deliver their message everywhere to all men (vv. 4 and 6). The Bible is squarely behind the argument that God's existence is manifestly declared in nature.

Romans 1:18-32 contains what may be the bitterest, most judgmental sentences in human speech. Here, the Bible declares that nature provides such strong testimony to God's existence, character, and attributes that men are universally rendered guilty and wrath-deserving, under the righteous judgment of God. This passage is a clear statement of the reason for pagan guilt, and the justification for Christian missions. A higher evaluation of the causal argument could hardly be imagined than that which Paul has provided in this passage.

Even apart from the other theistic arguments, this evidence ought to make men ask questions about God. It has always had an important place in preparing the hearts of men to believe the Gospel. David asked, "He that planted the ear, shall He not hear? He that formed the eye, shall He not see? He that chastiseth the heathen, shall not He correct? He that teacheth man knowledge, shall not He know?" (Ps. 94:9-10)

One of the great names of British science, mathematics, and philosophy is Sir Isaac Newton (1642-1727). Sir Isaac had a miniature model of the solar system made. A large golden ball representing the sun was at its center and around it revolved smaller spheres, representing the planets—Mercury, Venus, Earth, Mars, Jupiter, and the others. They were each kept in an orbit relatively the same as in the real solar system. By means of rods, cogwheels, and belts they all moved around the center gold ball in exact precision. A friend called on the noted man one day while he was studying the model. The friend was not a believer in the biblical doctrine of divine creation.

According to reports, their conversation went as follows:

Friend: "My Newton, what an exquisite thing! Who made it for you?"

Newton: "Nobody."

Friend: "Nobody?"

Newton: "That's right! I said nobody! All of these balls and cogs and belts and gears just happened to come together, and wonder of wonders, by chance they began revolving in their set orbits with perfect timing."

Of course, the visitor understood the unexpressed argument: "In the beginning God created the heaven and the earth."

We want to turn now to two other arguments for the existence of God. These also rest on the principle that there must be a cause for every effect.

Argument from Design

The argument from the presence of order in nature is also called the Argument from Design or the Teleological (from Greek *telos,* end, goal) Argument. There is a major premise in this argument: When orderly arrangement pervades a system it implies intelligence and purpose in the cause of the system. Since we can observe order in the universe, there must have been at the beginning of the universe an intelligence sufficient to design that order and purpose.

This major premise expresses a primitive and universal conviction. When, for example, we find a material object apparently made to be used for some purpose, say a stone axe, we feel certain that some man (intelligence) made it to cut wood (purpose). Both the intelligence and the purpose lie in the maker. We see unmistakable order all about us in nature. We know man did not make these features of his world. We know that only a Being with adequate intelligence to plan this system and with power to create it could cause it and did indeed cause it.

The major premise is a conviction shared by all mankind. We cannot conceive of a universe (that is, a world of many things harmonized in working unity) of weather, soil, water, temperature, animate and inanimate life existing apart from One who designed it for these ends. Why not call Him God?

Some men object that utter lack of purpose can also be seen in nature. Does evil have a purpose? Can God be the Author of a universe where pain and calamity are as prevalent as they are in our universe?

The Bible declares that evil does indeed have a place in the world of God's providence (see Gen. 50:5-21; Acts 2:22-24). God has designed it for human discipline. Evil, especially moral evil, remains a problem of thought, but it is not a barrier to faith.

Argument from Man's Nature

The argument from the nature of man is also called the Moral Argument or the Anthropological Argument.

We observe that men of all races, in all places, and of every social condition have a sense of right and wrong. They make moral judgments. If someone says it is wrong for men to have a sense of right and wrong, then he has made a judgment of right and wrong and seems inconsistent.

John Gerstner has written, "As intellectual beings we judge that certain things are right or wrong, but with that judgment always comes the notion that what we judge to be right, we *ought* to judge to be right; and what we judge to be wrong we *ought* [italics mine] to judge to be wrong" (*Reasons for Faith,* Harper, 1960, p. 39). Men everywhere agree that it is wrong to oppose a correct judgment of fact and conversely it is right to support it. If we do otherwise we feel an inner sense of wrongdoing. Something within accuses and threatens us.

We call that something *conscience*—a moral sense that accompanies knowledge of right and wrong. It supplies no information. And the information on which it passes judgment may be incorrect. But nevertheless, conscience tells us we *ought* to do what is right regarding the information we have. This sense of *duty* may be weak (1 Cor. 8:12), good (1 Peter 3:16), defiled (1 Cor. 8:7), seared (1 Tim. 4:2), strong or pure (1 Cor. 8:7; 1 Cor. 8:9). But it is never absent.

The only adequate explanation is that the great Moral Being, who created us all, planted the moral sense in us. No other explanation is adequate.

3

How God Revealed Himself to Men

"God spake in time past" (Heb. 1:1).

Stories told of two very different people set before us the subject of this study. One is the late Bertrand Russell (1872-1970), English nobleman, philosopher, mathematician, writer, and radical political personality. Russell was an articulate and often bitter disbeliever in God. It is reported that at a certain social gathering a Christian lady asked him a question, "Lord Russell, if, after you die, you come before God Almighty as Judge of the world, what will you say to Him?" The famous man remained silent for only a moment and then replied, "I shall address God and say, 'Sir, you did not make yourself plain.'"

The other person is the famous American lady, Helen Keller (1880-1968). From the age of two, Miss Keller was blind, deaf, and without the sense of smell. She received an ingenious and imaginative training and she responded so remarkably that the whole world wondered at the accomplishments of tutors and tutored. Sometime after she had progressed to the place where she could engage in conversation she was told of God, the Father of our Lord Jesus Christ. She is said to have responded with joy, "I always knew He was there, but I didn't know His name." As is generally known, Miss Keller became a devout and committed Christian.

Can We See the Invisible God?

When we say that God has revealed Himself, we do not mean that any man or angel has ever seen that infinite and eternal Spirit whom we call God. No man can see God and live (Ex. 33:20). "No man hath seen God at any time" (John 1:18). Yet the Bible declares that certain persons had special meetings with God; Isaiah, for example, and Moses. We call these disclosures of God *revelations*.

Both Scripture and sound theology mean by *revelation* the "making known of information." It may be a statement of fact ("In the beginning God created the heaven and the earth") or an announcement of some abstract truth ("righteousness exalteth a nation"). It may take the form of a command ("Thou shalt not commit adultery"), a narrative of past events (the dedication of the temple), or a prediction ("Your God shall come"). Sometimes such revelation is Spirit-guided human reflection on spiritual experiences ("The Lord is my Shepherd, I shall not want"). "In Christian theology the doctrine of revelation is the doctrine of God's making Himself, and relevant truths about Himself, known to man" (J. O. Buswell, *A Systematic Theology of the Christian Religion,* Zondervan, 1962, I, p. 183).

Revelation Both Probable and Necessary

That God should make Himself known to mankind is antecedently *probable*. The intrinsic probability of revelation from a God such as the Bible describes is illustrated in a story I once heard. A women from a tribe that had never heard the Gospel listened carefully while the missionary told the grand story of God's love. As the missionary closed, the tribeswomen said, "I always thought there ought to be a God like that." The spiritual hunger of people everywhere witnesses to the need for divine revelation and thereby to the probability of it.

Something in man makes revelation not only helpful and appropriate but also *necessary* if he is to be fully happy. This is illustrated by the stories of Bertrand Russell and Helen Keller.

According to the Bible, from the time of the Fall in Eden, God has sought to make Himself known to man. Let us look at the means and modes of revelation God employed.

The New Testament says that in Old Testament times God spoke through prophets (Heb. 1:1). But how did He speak to the prophets? The text simply says, In many ways. What were some of them? By what means did Cain and Abel learn that the worship of God requires sacrifice? If Enoch walked with God and pleased Him, how did Enoch know what God wanted from him? If, as Paul says, the heathen suppress certain known truths about God before any missionary even finds them (Rom. 1:18), what is the content of their knowledge of God and how do they apprehend it?

The Spirit Teaches Men to Seek God

In the first place, there is strong evidence in the Bible that the Holy Spirit, who now in a very special way is convicting men of sin; has always striven with men. He has urged men "that they should seek God, if perhaps they might grope for Him and find Him" (Acts 17:27, NASB).

We do not know that this ever led men to true religion. Some peoples have embraced monotheism, as far as we know, without contact with biblical revelation. Doesn't the enormous paraphernalia of worship in the false religions in the world have at least this much realized truth at its root: If God *is,* He must not be ignored, but worshiped?

Some Bible scholars have argued from John 1:9 that Christ the eternal Word has always been lighting every man "coming into the world." We cannot be sure of that interpretation but we are sure that God's Spirit has always been in the world. Through what some teachers call God's *common grace,* the Spirit influences men for good and restrains evil.

The Light of Nature

God has also revealed Himself through the "heavens and earth" which He has made. The older writers call this "the light of nature."

The Bible is clear. Nature does have something to say to men about their Creator. Some of these statements are in the poetry of the Psalms. Psalm 104 speaks of the light as God's garments (v. 2), of the shafts of light shining through them as beams of His chamber (v. 3). The winds are God's messengers and the lightning His ministers (v. 4). The rest of the Psalm declares that all creation, including man, is God's work (vv. 24, 31). The Psalmist's reflections on nature bring to his mind God's greatness, His honor, His majesty (v. 1) His manifold wisdom, His great riches (v. 24), and His eternal glory (v. 31).

God apparently takes special joy in His works in nature. Just as man, made in God's likeness, rejoices in doing and making things, so the Creator rejoices eternally in His works.

The discerning believer, by means of this revelation, understands his dependence on God and the importance of praise and worship of God while life lasts (v. 33).

David composed many of the Psalms that treat the subject of God's revelation in nature. David, the shepherd and king, fed sheep, saw stars at night, and planted his feet on the rocky soil. He witnessed the nightly parade of God's material accomplishments in earth and sky, and wrote Psalm 19.

We learn from Paul's Epistle to the Romans that God holds men responsible for these truths: "For the wrath of God is revealed from heaven against all ungodliness and unrighteousness of men, who suppress the truth in unrighteousness, because that which is known about God is evident within them, for God made it evident to them. For since the creation of the world His invisible attributes, His eternal power and divine nature, have been clearly seen, being understood through what has been made, so they are without excuse. For even though they knew God, they did not honor Him as God, or give thanks; but they became futile in their speculations, and their foolish heart was darkened. Professing to be wise, they became fools, and exchanged the glory of the incorruptible God for an image in the form of corruptible man and of birds and four-footed animals and crawling creatures" (Rom. 1:18-23, NASB).

Rational human beings are responsible to respond righteously to the knowledge God has imparted. But they do not. On the contrary, they suppress the truth (v. 18). Though they know God is invisible they make images and worship them, as if God were visible like mortal men and brute animals. Men are therefore "without excuse" (v. 20) and "the wrath of God is revealed" [in Scripture and conscience] against them. God releases them to follow out their unrighteous decisions: "God gave them over" (v. 24); "for this reason God gave them over to degrading passions" (v. 26); "And just as they did not see fit to acknowledge God any longer, God gave them over to a depraved mind, to do those things which are not proper" (v. 28, NASB).

What then is the content of nature's message about God? It tells of His greatness, His honor and majesty. It displays His wisdom, His riches and great glory. Such revelations teach also the utter inappropriateness of sin and of sinners in God's world. They have no rightful place here. While the message of God's greatness, honor, and majesty brings pleasure to redeemed people, it is bad news to sinners. It leaves them without excuse.

The gifts of sun, wind, rain, fertile soil, and fruitful seasons fill men's "hearts with food and gladness" (Acts 14:17), and ought to bring men to repentance (Rom. 2:4), but sadly they do not (Rom. 2:5).

The Light of Conscience

Man's own personal, rational and moral nature has been another means God has employed in speaking to the sinful race.

Certain philosophers, from ancient times, have launched their search for ultimate truths by looking into their own hearts and minds. "Know thyself" (Socrates) and "I think, therefore I am" (Descartes) are well-known expressions of this method.

John Calvin, who so greatly influenced Protestant theology in America, wrote at the opening of his great work of doctrine, of the response of a regenerate and sanctified logic: "No one can look upon himself without immediately turning his thoughts to contemplation of God in whom he 'lives and moves' [Acts 17:28]. For, quite clearly, the mighty gifts with which we are endowed are hardly from ourselves; indeed, our very being is nothing but subsistence in the one God. Then by these benefits shed like dew from heaven upon us, we are led as by rivulets to the spring itself" (*Institutes,* I 1.1).

Calvin's logic is correct, but it is regenerate, sanctified logic, informed by Scripture. Scripture speaks of man's being, his rational and moral nature, as a source of common knowledge of God. Man was created in God's likeness. The image of God is chiefly, though certainly not exclusively, man's personal, rational, and moral nature. Though marred by the Fall and, as to holiness and love for God, wholly spoiled, the image remains. Precisely because all men possess that image, murder of another man is a heinous crime (Gen. 9:6). For the same reason, slander or malicious cursing of other men is vicious iniquity (James 3:8-10).

Paul wrote: "For when Gentiles who do not have the Law do instinctively the things of the Law [Moses' Law], they show the work of the Law written in their hearts, their conscience bearing witness, and their thoughts alternately accusing or else defending themselves, on the day when . . . God will judge the secrets of men through Christ Jesus" (Rom. 2:14-16, NASB).

Moral standards are written on men's hearts. They know right from wrong and they know they ought to do right. When they act in a manner which their own standards approve they have a good, nonaccusing conscience. Conversely, when they violate their own standards they feel accused by a painful conscience. They sense the sanctions of a righteous God threatening them on the Judgment Day.

Thus, men everywhere *can* know and we may presume generally *do* know that like themselves, God is a moral Being, that unlike themselves, He is entirely righteous. On other grounds they know Him to be Creator and hence moral Governor of all men. Therefore, they expect a Judgment Day when they must face God, even though they fear Him.

It is now time to pause for certain reflections. We have discovered nothing thus far that clearly informs men that God is gracious. No light of nature or prompting of conscience says that

He has redeemed men, or even that God loves them. Nature threatens as much as it smiles and no prosecutor or judge can be more unrelentingly antagonistic than a guilty conscience. We turn now to some of the ways God has conveyed His message of love, grace, and redemption.

Primitive Revelation

God has made Himself known to men of all generations through original (or primitive) and direct revelation. When some men still "walked with God" (Gen. 5:22; 6:9) and conversed with Him (Gen. 3:8—4:15), He made this revelation.

"The Bible indicates that God revealed Himself to mankind at the beginning of human history, and that He hath not left Himself [in any age or place] without a witness (Acts 14:16-17). There is corroborative data in the study of comparative religions and cultural anthropology, indicating that the oldest religious traditions are the nearest to biblical theism. The scriptural teaching on primitive revelation [namely, original and direct] must be considered as a factor in the convicting work of the Spirit. There is generally among primitive peoples some trace or tradition of knowledge of the true God" (J. O. Buswell, *Systematic Theology,* II, pp. 159-160).

Some modern psychological theories emphasize an innate memory of race experience. The Bible neither affirms nor denies this. Human culture preserves ancient knowledge in ways we are scarcely aware of. But let me cite an example. There is in the Culver family an interesting tradition at least 1,300 years old, though I discovered it only recently. My father's given name was Cyniard. He never liked the name and always wondered where it came from. He knew that he was named for a distant relative of his grandfather's generation but he did not know that he was English, an eleventh generation American Culver (thirteenth through a female branch) and that the family name is an old Saxon name meaning "dove."

My wife and I took a month's tour of Britain in 1973. As we traveled along I read the three volumes of Trevelyan's *History of*

England. Imagine my excitement when in reading the first volume I found the name, Cyniard, attached to a young king of the Saxon kingdom of Mercia (in Great Britain). The mystery was solved—at least for me. A fragment of culture from our ancestors in continental Saxon Germany still survives in the fact that a grandson and a great-grandson bear my father's first name. We can pass traditions on for thousands of years without knowing it. Perhaps most of the best ideas men have about God have come to us in this way.

Revelation Through God's Acts

God has revealed Himself in special providential and miraculous works. Sometimes we do not know if some extraordinary event falls in the category of God's ordinary working (the laws of nature) or His special working (miracles). The distinction between *natural* and *miraculous* is valid, and in either case, what God does says something about who and what He is. Some claim that it was a landslide that cut off the waters of the Jordan when the Israelites passed through, and that a natural wind parted the Red Sea. Scripture says an east wind had something to do with parting the waters of the Red Sea. But in both cases God's omniscience and omnipotence were at work. We truly do not know *how* God works, either in miracles or in providence. In many cases we do know *why*.

We do not know whether the first plagues of Egypt came from natural causes or not; their timing certainly did not. Several of them were distinct miracles. God's power operated for special reasons. One of the reasons was to teach something to Pharaoh and all the nations who heard the report of the plagues. Pharaoh had said, "Who is the Lord, that I should obey His voice?" (Ex. 5:2) But the Lord said, "And I . . . will multiply My signs and My wonders in the land of Egypt . . . and the Egyptians shall know that I am the Lord, when I stretch forth My hand upon Egypt" (Ex. 7:3, 5).

God wanted Pharaoh and all of his people to learn something about the Lord. Moses said to the Egyptian king during one of the plagues, "I will spread abroad my hands unto the Lord; and the thunder shall cease, neither shall there be any more hail; *that thou mayest know* how that the earth is the Lord's" (Ex. 9:29, italics added).

The people of God of that generation and all later generations were to be taught about God by those events: "And the Lord said unto Moses, 'Go in unto Pharaoh; for I have hardened his heart, and the heart of his servants, that I might shew these signs before him; and that thou mayest tell in the ears of thy son, and of thy son's son, what things I have done in Egypt, and My signs [miracles] which I have done among them; *that ye may know* how that I am the Lord' " (Ex. 10:1-2, italics added).

Throughout biblical and Christian history, God's people have learned many things about their God through the biblical miracles and providences of God. The prophets frequently rebuked Israel for forgetting about them or misinterpreting them. (Other Scripture passages which discuss this matter are Deut. 4:33-35; Josh. 4:23-24; Isa. 45:1-6; Ex. 11:9-10; John 10:38; Ps. 105; 106:7-15).

Israel learned from these events that their God never fails to keep a promise. They learned of God's providences that "The judgments of the Lord are true and righteous altogether" (Ps. 19:9). And we may be sure that God still reigns. By His reign He taught England and France through the Battle of Waterloo. And He is teaching today's nations through the great wars of the twentieth century. God speaks to us also through wild flowers and the discoveries of science. As Tennyson wrote in 1869,

Flower in the crannied wall,
I pluck you out of the crannies,
I hold you here, root and all, in my hand.
Little flower—but *if* I could understand
What you are, root and all, and all in all,
I should know what God and man is.

Scriptural Revelation

God reveals Himself in a special way through the Holy Scripture. The Bible is a perfect revelation "that the man of God may be perfect, throughly furnished unto all good works" (2 Tim. 3:17). Several observations about the Bible as a source of truth about God are important to us.

The Bible claims to be not one message, but a series of messages about God. These messages begin with the earliest prophetic deliverances of the Old Testament and continue through the last of our Lord's apostolic witnesses (Heb. 1:1-2; 2:1-4). The Gospel of Christ was promised in the Old Testament (John 5:39, Rom. 1:1-3), fulfilled and spelled out very plainly in the New (Rom. 1:15-17; see also Luke 24:25-27, 44-47). The Scriptures are a *complete* guide to what we must believe to be saved, as well as all the information we need for dedicated service and holy living (2 Tim. 3:16-17).

There is also imponderable, mysterious power in the Scriptures in the vernacular language of any people. When made known by preaching and reading, that power will convert and redeem individual persons while also improving and refining their morals, manners, economy, and material culture (Rom. 10:9-17; Heb. 4:12; 1 Peter 1:23-25).

God Revealed in Jesus Christ

Finally, God has revealed Himself uniquely in His Son, the second member of the Godhead, our Lord Jesus Christ. His name, *Immanuel*, means "God with us" (Isa. 7:14). He is "the Mighty God" (Isa. 9:6). John wrote: "the Word has made flesh and dwelt among us, (and we beheld His glory, the glory as of the only begotten of the Father,) . . . no man hath seen God at any time; the only begotten Son, which is in the bosom of the Father, He hath declared Him" (John 1:14, 18).

This revelation stands apart from all others. Christ is the end of our search, the consummation of our hope for finding God or of His finding men. He provides a *perfect* revelation in that it is both complete and final. When God had spoken through our Lord there was nothing more to say. So the risen, ascended Christ "sat down on the right hand of the Majesty on high" (Heb. 1:3; see Col. 2:9, John 14:8-19; 16:12-15).

We shall learn more of our Lord when we see Him face to face, for there is more of His grace yet to be revealed (1 Peter 1:13), but God has no new avenues of revelation to open. In a certain way this is true of the Scriptures too. There are no new verses or chapters to be written, but it is possible every time I read the Bible or hear it expounded that I may notice a fact new to me or gain fresh insight into truth only dimly perceived before.

As we reflect on the variety of means and modes of learning about God discussed in this chapter it becomes apparent that very little of God's grace and redemption are known to us apart from the last three mentioned: God's providential and miraculous works, the Scriptures, and Jesus Christ. The other sorts of revelation, each valid in some circumscribed way, are inadequate; they are partial and obscure. All of them must be tested and judged by Scripture. Each achieves a normative, dependable status only as interpreted by Scripture. The Bible and Christ alone are complete and perfect, while only Christ speaks in a final way of God.

In an important sense, all revelation is by Jesus Christ, the "Author and Finisher of our faith," for He provided all the others. He is the Creator of the universe and man (John 1:1-3). He is the Giver of that original revelation and He shaped the experiences of Israel through providence (see 1 Cor. 10:1-3). And finally, He gave us the Bible (1 Peter 1:10-11).

The only truly *authentic* report we have of the person and redeeming work of Christ is found in the Bible. Without the Holy Scriptures we could know no truth unmixed with error. So, even though our faith for salvation is wholly in Christ, we learn of Him in the Bible: "Jesus loves me, this I know. For the Bible tells me so!" And though Christ said, "If any man hear My voice and open the door, I will come in to him" (Rev. 3:20), the voice with which He speaks is always in the words of Holy Scripture. And, amazingly, throughout our lives the Bible seems to speak in the language of the particular translation in which we first heard and read the Scripture.

4

The Spirituality of God

"God is Spirit" (John 4:24).

Let us go back to a junior high school science class. The teacher brings to the desk a beaker three-fourths full of an unknown substance. He holds it up so that all in the room can see it. It is a clear liquid. Is it methyl alcohol? No, for it has no odor at room temperature. So now we know it is an odorless, clear liquid.

Does it taste like any known clear liquid? No, it is tasteless as well as odorless. Further testing over the Bunsen burner shows that it boils at $+212°$ F. and the teacher says it turns to solid state at $+32°$F. The teacher also tells the class that it has been shown to be composed, by weight, of 11.188 percent hydrogen and 88.812 percent oxygen and nothing more. By now every child in the class knows for sure what the substance is. Water.

How is water defined? By its characteristics or *attributes*. And how do we identify it? The same way.

We have now reached a point in our study of God where it is appropriate to discuss His *attributes*. Though there is a text of Scripture (Isa. 40:18) which teaches that God cannot be likened to anything, when we speak of God's attributes we are answering the question, What is God like?

Just as a look at a road map of a territory we want to visit helps us to understand particular points of interest before we actually see them, so a classification of God's attributes will help us at this point. There is a classification based on a distinction between what God is in Himself (*absolute* or *immanent* attributes) and what He is in relation to creation (*relative* or *transitive*). It is a helpful classification and the usual one employed by writers on systematic theology.

All who seek to analyze and arrange such ideas a life, person, holiness, omnipotence, spirit, and others in the biblical sources are bound to struggle for clarity and consistency. I have chosen, for the sake of interest and simplicity, to use five biblical affirmations as captions for the arrangement. This has the advantage of making the Bible our authority for the ideas apparent. These affirmations are: *first,* "God is Spirit" (John 4:24, NASB); *second,* "The Lord He is God in heaven above, and upon the earth beneath; there is none else" (Deut. 4:39); *third,* "Great is our God above all gods" (2 Chron. 2:5); *fourth,* "O give thanks unto the LORD, for He is good" (Ps. 107:1); *fifth,* "In the name of the Father, and of the Son, and of the Holy Ghost" (Matt. 28:19).

In this chapter we will consider the spiritual nature of the Godhead under the first of these five biblical rubrics, "God is Spirit" (John 4:24, NASB).

"God is Spirit," a saying of Jesus, was spoken for practical reasons. In conversation with the woman at the well, Jesus spoke of an age in which geographical location and physical elements of worship are no longer important. Whatever temporary value the Old Testament ritual and materials may have had, they are now worthless. They may teach us but we dare not perpetuate them.

"God is Spirit," Jesus said, "and they that worship Him must worship in spirit and in truth." True worship is in the spiritual realm. However much man's unity of body and spirit and his residence in a material world may require such things as buildings, music, hymn books, Bibles, pews and central heating, ceremonies, and religious objects, these things are now secondary to the purely spiritual. We are free from any elaborate ceremonial system, any "yoke upon the neck of the disciples which neither our fathers nor we were able to bear" (Acts 15:10).

No one has ever framed a fully satisfying definition of *spirit*. For those who believe that matter and the chemistry of it are only part of reality, holding that there is nonmaterial reality, the following should be adequate. *Spirit is a nonmaterial, personal reality*.

The Bible presents God as self-conscious personal Spirit. He is the living God, active and intelligent. He is not only a God who acts freely (self-determination) but with sovereign purpose. It is this group of ideas we must think of when we say: God is Spirit.

It is impossible to isolate these elements completely, even for purposes of discussion. Some of the ideas group themselves together more closely than others. In the first group are personality, self-consciousness, and freedom (or self-determination).

Personality

A person is a subject who thinks, as well as being an object of thought. By this we mean that there is a kind of relationship unique to persons. I address *thee* (to employ the old second person singular form). I am *thou* to *thee* and thou art *thou* to *me*. This is unique to persons. Anything else with which I relate myself as a person is an *it*. Of course, when I talk about *thee* with another *thou,* then thou art a *he* or *she,* for purposes of discourse.

Such a description gives us an example of how personality works, rather than what it is. We know ourselves to be persons. From the way the Bible speaks of God—always an *I* addressing a *thou* or *you* (plural) and referring to *him* or *them*—we know that God is also a person.

We only need to trace these relationships through a fragment of the biblical evidence to be convinced. God is never a distant impersonal ghost, sounding impersonally through some occultist medium; nor is He an eternal spook regulating the fall of dice from some priest's hands. He is always a great Person.

For example, in Genesis 3:9-23 the personal character of God is as plain as that of Adam and Eve. Moses' meeting with God at the burning bush is no meditation of some pious sheepherder upon the magnificence of a sunrise or a sunset, but a sustained, sometimes fierce, conversation between two persons (Ex.

3:1—4:17). Nor were the events at Sinai some sort of natural volcanic eruption, as unbelief sometimes insists. When God addressed the whole nation, He spoke in personal modes (Ex. 19:9-19; Deut. 4:8-13; 18:16).

So when we say that God is a Person, before all else, we mean that he is the God of Holy Scripture, One who addresses us in Scripture and in sermon, One who sometimes spoke in the ages of revelation in audible ways to other persons, apostles and prophets. Biblical personalities interacted with Him—Adam and Eve, Abraham, Moses, Samuel, Isaiah and many others. In a less distinct, but equally important manner, we respond to Him in love, obedience, devotion, worship, prayer and service. Men of old sometimes conversed with Him. One of them, in fact, became so intimate with God that men came to call him "The Friend of God."

Once in Scripture, God called Abraham "My friend" (Isa. 41:8). King Jehoshaphat, in addressing God, referred to Abraham as "Thy friend" (2 Chron. 20:7) and James wrote that Abraham was called "the friend of God" (James 2:23).

This relationship between God and Abraham grew as do all friendships—between persons who share their interests. Once, God was on His way to destroy Sodom and Gomorrah. He stopped by Abraham's tent to talk business, urgent business, with him. While they ate (Gen. 18:8) and talked (Gen. 18:9-18) they took care of certain matters. Abraham received the announcement that Sarah would have a child, who would be the means of blessing to the whole world (Gen. 17:1-2). Within a year, Isaac would be born.

After this—and before the angel of the Lord went on to destroy the cities of the plain—the Lord said, "Shall I hide from Abraham that thing which I do?" (Gen. 18:17) So God affirmed His abiding confidence in Abraham and bared His heart. He told the patriarch of His plan to destroy the cities. He treated Abraham like an intimate friend. The rest of the chapter narrates the conversation, very significantly closing: "And the Lord went His way as soon as He had left communing with Abraham: and Abraham returned unto his place" (Gen. 18:33).

The God of the Bible is a Person—so much a Person that one man of history became His confidant—the friend of God. To this day Muslim Arabs refer to the great building over the cave of Machpelah near Hebron as *el Khalil,* "The Friend." The title reflects their reverence for Abraham's connection with the place (Gen. 23).

Self-consciousness

Self-consciousness is a second element of what it means to be a person. Sometimes, by twisting language, we refer to animals as if they were persons. We may even address them as persons and we fondly imagine that they respond. But in a lucid moment no person believes an animal to be self-conscious.

Animals are conscious, of course. They go to sleep and awaken. They receive sensations and respond to them. But man has the ability to think of himself objectively, engaging in introspection as he does. We are aware of our own actions and states of mind and we can rationally distinguish the self which is the subject of those states of mind and which initiates the actions. Brutes cannot accomplish these feats of personal beings. "In consciousness the object is another substance than the subject; but in self-consciousness the object is the same substance as the subject" (W. G. T. Shedd, *Dogmatic Theology I,* Zondervan, p. 179).

This truth is one aspect of the famous declaration of God to Moses as He responded to Moses' questions, What is Your name? "I AM THAT I AM . . . say to the sons of Israel, I AM has sent me" (Ex. 3:14, NASB). Here is the ultimate self-conscious Person.

God's self-consciousness, like all other features of His being, is His in perfection. I am unconscious of innumerable crannies of my personality. I do not wish to acknowledge some of these even when others who see them point them out to me. "Who can discern his errors?" David wanted to know. He prayed: Acquit me of hidden [i.e., hidden from myself] faults" (Ps. 19:12, NASB). And more at length, "Search me, O God, and know my heart: try me and know my thoughts" (Ps. 139:24).

God completely knows Himself. He is never surprised at what He says or does. So it was with our Saviour in the days of His flesh (John 6:6). Since this is so, we may ask our God to help us discover ourselves and the deep things of God. We need His Spirit to give meaning to the things of redemption. He knows the deep things of God (1 Cor. 2:9-10). "The things of God knoweth no man, but the Spirit of God. Now we have received, not the spirit of the world, but the Spirit which is of God; that we might know the things that are freely given to us of God" (1 Cor. 2:11-12).

Freedom or Self-determination

Freedom is a third element of God's personal, spiritual existence. All things we can think of are determined in some way by the characteristics of their own natures. Material elements are determined by that implanted nature science discovers when it determines what an object will do under certain conditions. Animals too have characteristics determined by their nature as brutes. Animal training is based on this. Human beings are also determined to a degree and our societal behavior is somewhat predictable. Politicians, social planners, and technocrats can manipulate us individually and collectively, up to a point, since they know we are determined by certain collective characteristics.

Men's responses, however, cannot be wholly "conditioned" by external management. We are also, within limits, self-determined. Totalitarian regimes run aground on man's unwillingness to yield determination of his behavior very long, except within the legitimate parameters of limited government.

The bad side of this self-determination is ungodly lawlessness. But the good side is precisely their Godlikness as free persons. At best, our self-determination is limited by God; at worst, it is dreadfully misused. We are, after all, a sinful race.

God alone is fully self-determined. No one tells Him what to do. He takes counsel only with Himself (Gen. 1:26).

The first chapter of Isaiah's famous *Book of Consolation* (Isa. 40—66) is heavily laden with this doctrine. First, the prophet promises his downtrodden people, "Behold the Lord God [Adhonai-Jehovah] will come" as Deliverer (Isa. 40:10). Then God's utterly independent self-determination is set forth in several questions: "Who [else] hath measured the waters in the hollow of His hand, and meted out heaven with the span, and comprehended the earth in a measure, and weighed the mountains in scales, and the hills in a balance? Who [else] hath directed the Spirit of the LORD, or being His counselor hath taught him? With whom took He counsel, and who instructed Him, and taught Him . . . the ways of understanding?" (Isa. 40:12-14) In each case the answer is, no one but God—*Adonai-Jehovah.*

In one important respect the Christian God is wholly different from the gods of the great oriental religions, namely Hinduism and its derivatives, Buddhism, Parseeism, and others. They have no personal, self-conscious, self-determining, active, self-moving, living center. The center of reality is impersonal, unconscious, unmoving, and certainly not alive. These religions are pantheistic. God—insofar as it is correct to speak of the central fact of their religion as God—is personal only in man or other spirits. Although the notion is not entirely consistent with their doctrines about escape from the wheel of finite existence, All (= God) is under the control of eternal, immutable laws. There is no rightful place for personality, freedom, or consciousness in God.

These aspects of the God of the Bible have imparted a certain vibrant, joyous tone to biblical religion wherever and whenever they appear. They engender a certain godly pride in being human beings and especially of being among the people of God.

The second group of attributes involved in the spiritual nature of God are life, activity, and intelligence.

Life

Our God is the living God. The Bible is explicit on this point. The phrase, *the living God,* appears in every section of the Bible from the Pentateuch, where we read, Israel "heard the voice of the living God" speaking from Mount Horeb (Deut. 5:26) to the Book of Revelation in which a flying angel has "the seal of the living

God," and God is described as one who "sits on the throne" (Rev. 7:2, 10, NASB).

As we examine these texts, it becomes apparent that *the living God* is associated with all God's other attributes and works and these acquire new lustre from the association, while they in turn throw light on the meaning of the phrase, *the living God* (A. H. Strong, *Philosophy and Religion,* Griffith & Rowland, 1912 p. 180).

One of these many texts explains why this attribute is basic to all others: "But the Lord is the true God, He is the living God, an everlasting King; at His wrath the earth shall tremble, and the nations shall not be able to abide His indignation. Thus shall ye say unto them, 'The gods that have not made the heavens and the earth, even they shall perish from the earth and from under these heavens' " (Jer. 10:10-11). God is angry with the nations because they have given worship to idols, idols supposedly indwelt by deities who are empty and vain (vv. 14-15). "There is no breath in them" (v. 14). God the Creator, on the other hand (v. 12), continues to show Himself the living God by preservation and providence (v. 13).

A survey of the passages dealing with this attribute shows that the God of the Bible is the living God in a number of ways: God is greatly to be feared. Except for the elect people of God who were prepared for the event at Sinai, no other people can even hear God's audible voice and live (Deut. 5:26)—It is a fearful thing to fall into the hands of the living God. This, again, is in contrast to the idols of the heathen for whom the true believer should have nothing but contempt (Jer. 10:1-15). Surely Paul had this passage in mind when he wrote to the Thessalonians that they had "turned to God from idols to serve the living and true God" (1 Thes. 1:9).

Because God lives, His people may confidently pursue the goals of His kingdom (Josh. 3:10, cf. 11-17). "The living God is among you, . . . He will without fail drive out . . . the Canaanites . . ." The living God also rescues His own from threats on their lives when it serves His purpose. Nebuchadnezzar discovered this (Dan.

6, esp. vv. 25-27). This is why the intrepid missionary preacher can safely minimize bodily exercises leading to fame and wealth, in favor of a missionary life full of privations (1 Tim. 4:8) "because we trust in the living God" (v. 10) who has given promise "of the life that now is, and of that which is to come" (v. 8).

Jesus is the Mediator of that life of God to us, since He alone is a Priest with "the power of an endless life" (Heb. 7:16). Having "life in Himself" (John 5:26), our Lord is truly "the Way, the Truth and the Life" for us (John 14:6). In heaven, where vision of His beatitude is plain, the "living creatures give glory and honor and thanks . . . to Him who lives forever and ever . . . and will worship Him who lives forever and ever" (Rev. 4:9-10, NASB).

Activity

This attribute is scarcely separable from the idea of life. Men intuitively discern action or possible action as an integral aspect of life. The flicker of an eyelid restores the hope of life to the loved ones of an unconscious person when it is uncertain if he is yet alive.

The God of Scripture, however, acts *effectually*. When He acts, He does so omnipotently. The infinitely great, eternal Spirit, whom Christians worship as the one, true, and living God, is willing and able to work. The Creator of the heavens and earth now sustains and rules them. He is able to step into the orderly process at any time, as He did when he raised Christ from the dead.

This doctrine refutes the notions of the *Deists,* who banish God from the world He created and sustains, and of the *Panthiests,* who teach that God is an impersonal force in the universe. The Christian God is the triune God—the Father, Son and Holy Spirit—who is "eternally independent" in "self-sufficient life." Creation is no necessity with Him; it is a free act enabling Him to be a God of love.

This doctrine also delivers us from the hopelessness of human life in a world controlled only by natural laws. The Maker of the laws of nature is a Person. Men cannot override or direct these laws, but for His mercy's sake, God can and did (at Calvary) and may in response to prayer.

Intelligence

By intelligence, we mean perception of facts as they are (knowledge), genuine awareness of the meaning of those facts (understanding), and ability to put all those facts in proper relation (wisdom). This attribute of God guards Christianity from certain ideas fatal to biblical faith.

On the one hand there is the doctrine that the world has no personal center, Creator or control, called God, only a certain substance, an "it," in which inhere eternal "principles" or "laws." In secularized Western lands, where Christianity has long held nominal allegiance of the majority, this doctrine usually appears in supposedly harmless guise. "It" is called "Nature" or "Mother Nature" or "Mother Earth."

On the other hand, pantheistic (all is God) religions deny distinct knowledge of particular things. A personal divine being is supposedly a retrogression from the utter nonparticularity of ultimate reality. Because particular knowledge is a denial of this ultimate, Hinduism, Buddhism, Theosophy, and Rosacrucianism insist that a God who knows is closer to the Christian idea of Satan than of our Lord Jesus' Holy Father. A Pantheist can find no comfort in David's assuring words, "Like as a father pitieth His children, so the Lord pitieth them that fear Him. For He knoweth our frame, He remembereth that we are dust" (Ps. 103: 13-14).

"Nature protects the groundhog in winter" or "Mother Nature teaches the birds where to make their nests" are statements utterly out of place in a Christian setting. For Christians the personal Creator remains in personal control of the whole order of creation. Psalm 104 is instructive. The psalmist describes the clouds, with shafts of light beaming through, as garments and chambers for Him, since He makes them (vv. 1-3). The winds and lightnings are His messengers (vv. 3-4). He holds the earth steady (v. 5) and covers the oceanic mountains with water (v. 6). The thunder is His voice (v. 7). God's personal *knowledge* insures nature's success, its magnificent rhythms and its cycles. "O Lord, how manifold are Thy works," the Psalmist wrote. "In wisdom hast Thou made them all" (v. 24).

The wisdom of the creatures of nature in their manifold life-processes, operating to preserve the order of nature in what we have come to call the ecological balance, is planted there by God. "The Lord by wisdom hath founded the earth; by understanding hath He established the heavens. By His knowledge the depths are broken up, and the clouds drop down the dew" (Prov. 3:19-20).

The God of Scripture is a God of knowledge (1 Sam. 1:3); His Spirit is "the spirit of wisdom and understanding, the spirit of counsel . . . , the spirit of knowledge" (Isa. 11:2). God challenges man: "Shall he that contendeth with the Almighty instruct Him?" (Job 40:2) The end of Job's debate came when the living, personal, knowing God simply overwhelmed him by His knowledge of nature and man's ignorance of it (Job 38—41). The only proper response was the one Job made—he repented in dust and ashes (Job 42:6). So it should be with today's scientists who challenge God's rightful place in nature, beneath nature, and above it. "Shall the work say of Him that made it, He made me not? or shall the thing framed say of Him that framed it, He had no understanding?" (Isa. 29:16)

But it is not in nature that God's wisdom shall be most fully revealed. The church of Christ, the household of faith in the one true living God, is yet to be the scene of the manifestation of that wisdom in spite of all her failures here below (Eph. 3:10, 21).

5

The Unity of the Godhead

"The Lord He is God in heaven above, and upon the earth beneath; there is none else" (Deut. 4:39).

A story coming out of the great economic depression of the 1930s illustrates the need for acceptable names for things. A city-bred college graduate got a job with a small town bank. He was in the loan department and was assigned the task of inspecting farms where the bank had lent the farmer money to operate his farm. The recruit was given pictures of the various animals customarily found on farms. He was to identify the animals with the use of the pictures. He was to count the animals on each farm and bring back a report. He had pictures of chickens, ducks, geese, turkeys, Jersey cattle, Holstein cattle, horses of various breeds, sheep and hogs. Somehow there were no pictures of goats.

Upon returning from his first inspection, the greenhorn inspector made his report—so many white hogs, so many brown ducks, and so on. But, he told his superior, "There was one critter I could not identify."

"What did it look like?" his boss wanted to know.

"Well," the confused young man said, "He was rather small and thin, had shaggy grey and black hair, a long mournful face and a small beard of chin whiskers." The boss, now thoroughly exasperated, impatiently cut in without allowing the young inspector to say how many legs the animal had or if it had a tail.

54

"You fool!" he said. "That is no animal. That is the farmer."

Terms are important. The student of the Christian faith must get acquainted with some of the special expressions for ideas about God.

Special Vocabulary for Study of Religions

Three terms are employed to describe what are usually thought to be the lowest forms of religion. The belief in the powers of charms and amulets—objects to bring good luck to the bearer and to ward off bad luck—is known as *dynamism* (from Greek *dynamis*, power). Such people think that some sort of nonmaterial (spiritual is hardly the word), but impersonal, power pervades everything, but especially the material object worn.

Fetishism is a refinement of dynamism. Fetishism holds that a powerful spirit inhabits some material object. Perhaps some good incident takes place in connection with a manmade object. The tribe then adopts the object and venerates it, even carrying it during migration or in warfare.

Animism is a belief in nature spirits—many of them. They inhabit streams, springs, trees, waterfalls, and mountains. The events of nature—storms, lightning, floods—are supposedly caused by them.

On a more "advanced" level of culture and presumably, therefore, one in which people are more reflective, there is a tendency "to universalize various types of phenomena and identify each with a particular deity such as a god of storms, another of harvest and another of procreation" (Harold DeWolf, *A Theology of the Living Church,* Harper, 1953, p. 89).

We are familiar with this in the classical *polytheism* of Greeks and Romans and in the less-publicized preliterate worship of the nations of Western and Northern Europe. This form of worship of many gods is memorialized in several of the days of our week, Thor in Thursday, Wotan in Wednesday, and in the months of the year, Juno in June, Janus in January, and Mars in March.

The Old Testament preserves fragments of ancient Near Eastern polytheism in the names of several gods and goddesses (Baal,

Hadad, Moloch, and Ashtoreth). Scholars disagree as to whether these deities represented a breaking up of the functions of nature from some more unified way of looking at things, or the personification of the multifarious powers of nature.

An invariable accompaniment of polytheism is *idolatry*, wherein an image of the god, thought to be the actual local seat of the god's person, is worshiped. The idol and the god are identified in the worshipers' thoughts, however stupid that might appear to men of insight such as Elijah, Jeremiah, Isaiah, and Paul.

On a more sophisticated level, there have been cases of a king designating a certain god as the only one worthy of worship, while still regarding the other deities of the nation and its neighbors as real. The worship of the sun-god at Thebes at a certain stage of Egypt's history (14th century B. C.) was an example. We call this *henotheism* (one among many).

Dualism regards matter and spirit (or mind) as eternally real principles. Nearly always, matter is evil, and spirit is good. Parseeism, the modern form of ancient Zoroastrianism, is mainly dualistic.

Pantheism regards all that exists as manifestations of a single impersonal substance or principle. Hinduism, Buddhism, and several cults of oriental origin—Theosophy, Rosacrucianism and Transcendental Meditation are pantheistic.

Deism affirms the sole existence of one Creator-God, wholly transcendent, having no present relation with creation. It is a belief of advanced civilizations, but there have been few fully consistent deists.

Monotheism is the worship of one Supreme Being, personal and ethical, above the world (transcendent) as Creator yet immanent in the world as its preserver and ruler. Judaism and Islam are, besides Christianity, the only historic monotheistic faiths and Islam barely qualifies.

Theism is a form of monotheism. As understood by Christian writers, theism includes the idea that God is self-revealing in miracles, in prophecy, and (in the case of Christian theism) in Jesus Christ our Lord.

Scholars inclined toward naturalistic interpretations of all faiths like to find examples of all these forms of religions in the growth of Israel's religion. They draw no distinction, for example, between Rachel's evident belief in the portable family idols and Israel's use of the portable ark of the covenant, or between Nebuchadnezzar's evident henotheism and Abraham's worship of the Most High God. Whatever may be said for the low level of perception of true worship among the Hebrews when God first delivered them from the pagan atmosphere of Ur and Haran (see Josh. 24:2), the *revealed* faith, the worship which the Bible from beginning to end inculcates, is monotheism and theism.

Why Believe in One God?

In chapter two we introduced some of the reasons for believing in God. We said little, however, about *why* we should believe in only one God. We want to look now at the evidences for the monotheistic faith of Christians.

Interestingly, antiquity provides many examples of monotheistic religion. One of the pharaohs of Egypt enforced the worship of the sun-god alone. *Theos,* the commonest Greek word for God, appears often in the singular form among the later Greek writers. Several philosophers expressed theoretical ideas close to monotheism: Xenophanes, Heraclitus, Anaxagoras, in addition to Socrates, Plato and Aristotle.

After Alexander the Great (4th century B. C.) the Greek civilizing influence grew strong everywhere and the Roman Empire brought stability. The upper classes of literate people were particularly exposed to the new ideas. Among them, faith in the polytheistic deities declined. The Greeks and the Romans pondered the possibility of one single, personal, Creator-God. All the rational proofs available to us were available to them also.

Harold DeWolf argues, "In the historic development of religion there is a tendency for thought to move in the direction of monotheism . . . It is no accident that as a religious people increase in knowledge, in powers of discipline, in systematic thought and depth of cultural experience they tend to move toward montheism" (DeWolf, *Theology*, pp. 89, 91). Is not this fact in itself strong evidence for the sole existence of one Creator-God, Lord of history? Consider the unlikelihood of the contrary development of history. The growth of civilization, education, and culture toward a climax in polytheism or animism is very unlikely and, as far as I know, without historical precedent.

The coherence of the material universe into a single system of cause and effect. This suggests rather forcefully that there is a single all-wise, all-powerful, everywhere-present, personal power behind it. The more science probes the minute and infinitesimally small, the more it appears that all matter and energy are aspects of a single cosmos. The same system of cause and effect prevails in the farthest researches into space. We do live then in a universe, not a "pluraverse" or a "multiverse." Men can rationally formulate causal laws which are valid everywhere. This makes it more reasonable to believe in one *prime mover* or *first cause* rather than in several.

The coherence of all authentic abstract truths in a single system. This provides further evidence that the God of creation is one. These abstract data exist quite apart from men who discover them. In the small business houses of China, people figure the bills of customers on a frame of parallel spokes on which wooden rings are moved. It is called an abacus. My paint salesman now uses a handheld electric calculator. My 82-year-old mother uses pencilled figures on paper to add up her bills. (I let my wife figure them out!) The data and results of mathematics (4×3; $10 + 2$; $20 - 8$; $72 \div 6$ all yield the number 12) are invariable and universal.

The same is true of formal logic as taught in the schools of philosophy, whether the classical system of Aristotle or modern symbolic logic. These are true laws of reality. They can be discovered and formulated but never invented. Deduction and induction are nothing but aspects of one all-inclusive system of abstract truth. Abstract truth underlying or accompanying all other truths is a universal network, existing in perfection. This system sets bounds and binds us all. There is no rational existence as man without submitting to it. We call men crazy who do not. If this system of universal abstract truth is attributable to the mind(s) that created us, is it not rational, within this system of rational truth, to attribute it to One rather than many?

A system of ethical ideals. Another argument is an extension of the anthropological or moral argument for the existence of God, viz.: there is a system of ethical ideals, adherence to which is necessary for any sort of order in any community from a simple partnership to a civilized world order. Loyalty to ideals and to legitimate human leaders is necessary to civil order; honesty to the flow of trade; truthfulness equally necessary to science or business; discipline of children to family, school, civil commonweal. The Old Testament Decalogue, though given by God at Sinai, is a kind of moral consensus, necessary to "the greatest happiness for the greatest number." Generally speaking, except for the prohibition of images in worship, the Ten Commandments are praised around the whole world. There is, indeed, beneath the multiplicity of rules concerning social life and rules of custom, a single system of moral law. These ideal norms are objective and real even though stated in different ways. The Golden Rule of Jesus, for example, can also be found in the teachings of several moral philosophers (Confucius, Socrates, Buddha, Santayana) of widely separated epochs and places. Does not this single, universal, accepted standard of human behavior argue forcefully for a single moral Mind, rather than several, for its cause?

The nature of religious devotion. The logic from the nature of religious devotion impels us toward the conviction that God is one. We are told in the Bible, of course, that we must love the Lord our God with the whole of our being. God allows no competitors. He is a "jealous God." Let us turn this fact upside down. Thoughtful, cultivated worshipers of deity, in any religion, are apt to assume that their god desires single-minded, whole-souled worship. They tend to become devotees of a single deity, even while appeasing competing deities. Schleiermacher (1768-1834), a most influential theologian, insisted that religious experience has an inner logic which, when developed, impels toward faith in a single divine Being. In this respect, he seems to have been right. There is, in this way, an argument from the very nature of religious devotion for a single object of worship.

The teaching of Scripture is on a totally different level. The sole existence of one, authentic, Creator-God is assumed from the opening statement—"In the beginning God created the heaven and the earth"—to the claim of the last chapter, "I am Alpha and Omega, the beginning and the end, the first and the last." Let us see how the biblical evidence stands, what it means, and what the consequences for our thinking and action are.

Evolution Toward Monotheism in the Bible?

Someone wants to know if we can't find in the Bible a beginning of low forms of religion and subsequent evolution toward monotheism. Isn't there evidence that some of the heroes and heroines of the early narratives, such as Abraham and Sarah, Isaac and Rebekah, Jacob and Rachel, Moses and his family, practiced lower forms of religion such as animism, dynamism, and fetishism? Did not the Hebrew people really slowly move from acknowledgment of the existence of lesser gods or polytheism through henotheism to the true monotheism of the great prophets of Israel?

Some scholars say Yes. They argue that Abraham's attention to the oaks of Mamre as a place to live implies belief that favorable spirits dwelt in those trees (animism). Isaac's well-known interest in certain springs and wells is cited as evidence of the same. When Jacob returned to the environs of Bethel, where his grandfather had spent some time, and rested his head on a stone for a pillow, did he not demonstrate an animism or even fetishism which believes in the good influence of the spirits in portable objects? The story of angels descending and ascending, though told in a good monotheistic framework, truly rests upon the animism and fetishism of Jacob's time, we are told.

This same line of argument insists that when "the Lord sought to kill" Moses at an inn in the desert (Ex. 4:24-26) on account of the neglect of circumcision of his son, Jehovah Himself behaved like a demon in the wilderness. This shows the superstition of the time and the low views of God. The Ark of the Covenant—just a gold-cased wooden box—is evidence of fetishlike faith. And, the many references to the object of Abraham's worship, as "the Most High God" implies acknowledgment of lesser deities. The language of the historical sections of the Old Testament, we are assured, in no wise denies the existence of the gods of fertility and of weather (Baal, Moloch, Hadad) of Israel's neighbors, only their rejection by Israel's best leaders as proper objects of devotion.

What can we say in response to these charges? First of all, the claims rest on no straightforward declarations of the Bible. The Bible *teaches* none of these things directly. They are inferences drawn from a so-called history of Israel reconstructed on evolutionary principles and nineteenth-century literary analysis. Some of them have been rendered incredible by twentieth-century findings of archaeology.

Many of the Israelites may have been more henotheistic than monotheistic. We know that some of Abraham's ancestral family practiced polytheism, as did many of the Children of Israel during their sojourn in Egypt (Josh. 24:2). On the other hand, while we cannot explore Abraham's mind, we do read of God's self-revelation as Almighty God (Gen. 17:2) and Abraham's assurance that his God was "Judge of all the earth" (Gen. 18:25). These are quite inconsistent with henotheism. Furthermore, "the Most High God" of Melchizedek and of Abraham (Gen. 14:18-19) was "possessor of heaven and earth." Thus, the alleged henotheism turns out on examination to be full-blown ethical theism, or monotheism.

The interpretations about Abraham's trees, Jacob's stone pillow, and the ark rest on slender evidence.

We may freely acknowledge that many good people of Old Testament times partially misunderstood their own religion. Idolatry and polytheism were a constant threat. Some Israelites were drawn to occult practices and raw heathenism (2 Kings 17:6-23; Deut. 18:9-14). But in no case does the Scripture for a moment even hint that the God of its pages is less than a personal

Creator, Sustainer, Governor, and moral Judge of all the earth and heaven.

Direct Biblical Affirmations of Monotheism

Usually, the Bible introduces the doctrine of God's unity in connection with some command or duty. The truth furnishes the motive power for human obedience.

In spite of attempts of certain biblical critics to put all references to monotheism late in Israel's history, the early statements in Scripture constitute a full, vigorous, and uncompromising affirmation of the substantial unity of the Godhead. They have never been superceded.

In Deuteronomy, Moses reminded Israel that the Lord showed them the miracles of deliverance from Egypt and the theophany at Sinai, "that thou mightest know that the Lord, He is God; there is none else beside Him" (Deut. 4:35). These words came in the context of Moses' dying exhortation to undying loyalty to Jehovah and His revealed faith. Moses went on to say: "Hear [Hebrew, *shema'*; hence, Shema] O Israel: The Lord our God is one Lord: and thou shalt love the Lord thy God with all thine heart, and with all thy soul, and with all thy might" (Deut. 6:4-5). There is only one God, so all worshipful love is due Him.

The theology of the poetical books of the Old Testament is profoundly and exclusively an ethical monotheism. Occasional reference to other deities such as "Who is like Thee among the gods?" must be interpreted in view of the uniform monotheism. We should understand them as references to *alleged* gods, much as Elijah ridiculed the non-god Baal, and taunted the Baalish prophets as if Baal existed (1 Kings 18:17-29).

The prophets of the Old Testament, Isaiah in particular, had a striking way of asserting the sole existence of the God of Israel. These spokesmen for the Lord pointed to His knowledge of the future and His power to communicate it to His servants, the prophets. Let us note some powerful examples.

"Thus saith the Lord the King of Israel, and His Redeemer the Lord of hosts: 'I am the first, and I am the last; and beside Me there is no God. And who, as I, shall call, and shall declare it?' " (Isa. 44:6-7) Verse six makes fulfillment of prophetic predictions a clear proof of God's sole existence as Lord of time. Is He not the Eternal Father? (Isa. 9:6)

In Isaiah 45:1-6 the coming of the Persian king Cyrus, 150 years later, in fulfillment of Isaiah's predictions of him, is offered as proof that "I am the Lord, and there is none else, there is no God beside Me: I girded thee [Cyrus], though thou hast not known Me: that they [men on earth] may know from the rising of the sun, and from the west, that there is none else" (45:5-6). The clear ethical duty is to believe God's prophets and their message of Jehovah's sole existence as God.

Mark 10:18-24 tells how Jesus employed the *Shema* (Deut. 6:4) to instruct a somewhat hypocritical, but inquiring, scribe in the duty of undivided love for God. In John 5:44, Jesus refers to the Deity as "the one and only God" (NASB), and in His high priestly prayer as "the only true God" (John 17:3).

From Paul, we learn that since God is "one God," there is only one way of salvation for all classes of men (Rom. 3:19, 30). Since there is only one God, the idols of the heathen are bogus deities (1 Cor. 8:4-5). And in an oft-recited benediction Paul invoked "the only God" (1 Tim. 1:17, NASB) as the only source of human happiness and as the end of all praise and honor. He employs the same doctrine to appeal for steadfastness in Christian duties (1 Tim. 6:16).

James cites the "one God" doctrine as worthy of faith (James 2:19) and Jude 4 speaks of the denial of the truth as reprehensible.

These are only selected texts which speak specifically to the point. The whole Bible breathes the atmosphere of worship and love for that "blessed and only Potentate, the King of kings and Lord of lords, who only hath immortality, dwelling in the light which no man can approach unto; whom no man hath seen, nor can see: to whom be honor and power everlasting. Amen" (1 Tim. 6:15-16).

The doctrine of biblical monotheism does not exclude the possibility that certain other objects of human discourse, real or supposed, may be called "gods." Idols worshipped as gods are called gods in the Bible and the supposed, but unreal, unseen deities of polytheism are also called gods (see 1 Cor. 8:4-5).

If we understand Paul correctly, even though the divine objects of the Greek-Roman pantheon have never existed, there are certain divinely created, but fallen, corrupt, evil, unseen spirits, called demons, who sometimes appropriate worship offered to idols. In 1 Corinthians 8 Paul specifically branded the heathen gods and lords of heathenism as unreal. Yet, he enlarged on the subject in chapter 10 by saying, "Look at the nation Israel: are not those who eat the sacrifices sharers in the altar? What do I mean then? That a thing sacrificed to idols is anything, or that an idol is anything? No, but I say the things which the Gentiles sacrifice, they sacrifice to demons, and not to God; and I do not want you to become sharers in demons. You cannot drink the cup of the Lord and the cup of demons" (1 Cor. 10:18-21, NASB).

Nor does the doctrine of monotheism exclude the possibility of more than one person in the Godhead, for Jesus Himself affirmed, "I and My Father are one" (John 10:30). How this can be true we will see in chapter 8.

Biblical Proofs of Monotheism

The Bible has its own ways of supporting this teaching. Certain events were employed at the time of the Exodus to establish Israel in monotheism.

First, there were the mighty works of God, properly called miracles, associated with Israel's deliverance from Egypt. Moses certified himself as a true messenger of the God of Abraham, of Isaac, and of Jacob by three remarkable *signs* (miracles). These are mentioned in Exodus 4:1-9: the changing of Moses' inert rod into a serpent; the changing of his normal hand to a white, leprous one and then back to normal again; the conversion of water from the Nile into blood. After these miracles, we read, "the people believed."

Later, a series of even greater miracles, which we call the 10 plagues, convinced Israel even further and made a similar impression even on the magicians of Egypt (see Ex. 7—12). This unique method was God's way of certifying messengers who announced the truth of the sole existence of the God of Israel.

The Lord's spokesmen also relied on prediction and its fulfillment to authenticate themselves and their message. Each of the miracles involved predictions and fulfillment.

Religious Values of Monotheism

Many religious values grow out of belief in monotheism. Today, we can notice the confusion in efforts to placate the demigods of occultism, or the alleged powers of Satan. People fear the strange, the dimly lighted, and the weird if the only omnipotent God is not in control of man and nature. "They sacrificed unto devils, not to God; to gods whom they knew not, to new gods that came newly up, whom your fathers feared not. Of the Rock that begat thee thou art unmindful, and hast forgotten God that formed thee" (Deut. 32:17-18).

We are assured by the Bible that there is a single God for all men. Therefore, even though these may be a "chosen people," God's ultimate goal is a blessing of "all the nations" (Gen. 12:1-3). The sinner in Russia or Albania is as loved by God as the sinner in Britain, the Netherlands, or Canada. The doctrine of racial equality before God rests, in part, on ethical monotheism.

Finally, the principle of the uniformity of nature, which makes true science possible, rests on this truth. It is no accident that the age of modern science had its origin and growth in Christian lands.

The Greatness of God

"Great is our God above all gods" (2 Chron. 2:5).

O Lord my God! when I in awesome wonder
  Consider all the worlds Thy hands have made,
I see the stars, I hear the rolling thunder,
  Thy power throughout the universe displayed,
Then sings my soul, my Saviour God to Thee;
  How great Thou art, how great Thou art!

This Swedish hymn, "How Great Thou Art," translated by Stuart K. Kline and popularized by George Beverly Shea, finds an answering chord in all Christian believers. But God is great in ways that far outstrip worlds, stars, thunder, and power throughout the universe.

The historic creeds have distilled the scriptural statements, and in timeless words have captured the greatness of God with a splendor which even the hymns do not match. One of them speaks of God as "a Spirit infinite, eternal and unchangeable in His being, wisdom, power, holiness, justice, goodness and truth." These are cool, abstract words of logical analysis. But we all need an appreciation of the reality beyond the words.

Nothing is more important for sound faith and life than an *understanding* of God's attributes. It is not enough to have a feeling for God or even a love for Him. We need an intellectual awareness of His characteristics. Ancient Israel was impressed by God's power. They trembled at God's thundering, trumpetlike voice and His fire at Sinai. But after a few months of camping on the spot they made a calflike image of God and worshiped it. They simply did not understand who God is and what He is like.

God's greatness stretches our thinking. As we come to know more of what God is like we will be able to serve Him better.

In this chapter we want to explore briefly: God's Self-existence, His Eternity, Immensity, Omnipresence, Omniscience, Omnipotence, and His Incomprehensibility.

Self-Existence of God

God is the ground of His own existence. His only necessity is the necessity of His own being. It is God's nature *to be*. Nothing else we can observe or conceive exists apart from some chain of causes. The more we learn of men, the crowning excellency on earth of God's creative art, the more we are aware of men's frailty and dependence. All beings, heavenly and earthly, except the first and final Cause, Himself, are dependent creatures. An endless succession of causes for the world is unacceptable to the human mind. Our heart and flesh cry out for the living God.

Scriptural statements: "I AM THAT I AM" (Ex. 3:14); "My name Jehovah" (Ex. 6:3). YHWH, *Jehovah,* the name which Jews will not speak, is God's self-affirmation, "I AM" ('Hwh) put in the third person, "He Is." The word translated "I AM" is not meant merely to connect the two parts of a sentence; it is a statement about existence. In his book *On the Trinity* (I. 1, 2), Augustine, greatest of the ancient Christian theologians, said that God alone is the One of whom it can be unequivocally and unconditionally said, "He Is." "The fountain of living waters" (Jer. 2:13). "The fountain of life: in Thy light shall we see light" (Ps. 36:9).

Practical benefits: The assurance that believers truly have eternal life arises from God's self-existence. "He that heareth My word," we read, "and believeth on Him that sent Me, hath everlasting life, and shall not come into condemnation but is passed from death [our condition by nature] unto life [our condition in Christ] . . . For as the Father hath life in Himself; so hath He given to the Son to have life in Himself" (John 5:24, 26). God's being is the ground of ours.

His power to create and sustain life also insures the stability of the world. It is His will to preserve it: "While the earth remaineth, seedtime and harvest, and cold and heat, and summer and winter, and day and night shall not cease" (Gen. 8:22). We may safely ignore the garish threats of extinction proposed in the pages of the Sunday newspapers, just as we do some of the less rational predictions of the environmentalists.

Eternity of God

God deals with the world in time, but He Himself cannot be measured by time. He is without beginning or ending yet is Himself the cause of all other existent things which have duration. Thus, we can say that time is real because it is in Him.

Another way of speaking of God's relation to time is, He is *above* time. It is not strictly true to say He lives in an "eternal now," as we occasionally read, for the past and future are present in God's mind as truly as the present. In one sense *now* is nothing more than a point or line which the future passes in becoming past. And God lives not in a line separating past from future, but in eternity. There is logical succession in God's thoughts, but no chronological succession, and since creation now exists in the succession of events, God sees them and knows them. Time is therefore *real* for God.

In a sense, even human beings may live above time. By reflecting on remembered things we are able to "live in the past" and by projecting present tendencies, causes, and movements into tomorrow we can "live in the future." *Believers,* by their very definition of that word, are "past oriented" in that their redemption is already provided, and "future oriented" in that the consummation is to come.

Scriptural statements: "Thou hadst formed the earth and the world, even from everlasting to everlasting, Thou art God" (Ps.

90:2). The Lord describes Himself as "the high and lofty One [transcendent] that inhabiteth eternity" (Isa. 57:15). Christ is the One by whom God "made the ages" (Heb. 1:2, Greek) and God is "the King eternal" (1 Tim. 1:17. See also Gen. 21:33, Deut. 33:27; Ps. 102:12; Rom. 1:20; Isa. 41:4; 1 Cor. 2:7; Rev. 1:8; 4:10).

Practical benefits. God is as youthful and strong today as when Abel was born. "Thy years shall not fail." "Thou art the same." There is a place of quiet rest, near to the heart of God precisely because "the eternal God is thy refuge, and underneath are the everlasting arms" (Deut. 33:27; see also Ps. 102:1-13; Heb. 1:5-12).

Swift to its close ebbs out life's little day,
    Earth's joys grow dim, its glories pass away;
Change and decay in all around I see—
    O Thou who changest not, abide with me.

Immensity of God

God's nature is not extended in space; He is without spatial dimension and yet in Him all things consist. He is the Creator of space. We can readily see that as eternity designates God's infinity in relation to time, immensity is God's infinity in relation to space.

Scriptural statements. "But will God indeed dwell on earth? behold, the heaven and heaven of heavens cannot contain Thee; how much less this house that I have builded?" (1 Kings 8:27) Was Solomon thinking of Genesis 1:1? We don't know, but it is clear that Paul, in discussing the dimensions of God's love, put "things present" and "things to come" (aspects of time) along with "height" and "depth" (aspects of space) among the "creatures" (Rom. 8:38-39).

Omnipresence of God

"God," A. H. Strong once wrote, "in the totality of His essence, without diffusion or expansion, multiplication or division, penetrates and fills the universe in all its parts" (A. H. Strong,

Systematic Theology, p. 279). We have already met this idea, less critically defined, under the immanence of God. The idea is hard for us to grasp because the mind finds difficulty in conceiving of ideas without images.

Even though God is pure Spirit, children and naive adults almost necessarily think of God in corporeal images. When, as a small child, I first read in the Bible that man is made in God's image and likeness, it never occurred to me to doubt that God looked something like my father. "It must be said . . . that it is better for children and the unlearned to think of God corporeally rather than to think of Him as unreal. Yet it is remarkable with what steadfastness the main stream of Christian thought has kept within the bounds of spiritual conceptions" (DeWolf, *Theology,* p. 98).

Scriptural statements. "Whither shall I go from Thy Spirit?" asked the psalmist. "Or whither shall I flee from Thy presence? If I ascend up into heaven, Thou art there: if I make my bed in hell [the grave], behold, Thou art there. If I take the wings of the morning, and dwell in the uttermost parts of the sea; even there shall Thy hand lead me, and Thy right hand shall hold me" (Ps. 139:7-10). This is the godly believer's appreciation of the divine omnipresence. God Himself says in Scripture: " 'Am I a God at hand,' saith the Lord, 'and not a God afar off? Can any hide himself in secret places that I shall not see him?' saith the Lord" (Jer. 23:23-24). This is the immensity of the God who fills the universe.

Christians must resist the temptation to think of God's omnipresence in any material, tangible sense. It is fatal to any true "religious" spirituality. All sorts of crass forms of mysticism grow in the soil of material conceptions of God's omnipresence. A college chapel speaker, now a well-known novelist, spoke once of feeling God in her bath water! Another Christian knew the Spirit was in a meeting because, said he, he felt the pressure of His power under his fifth rib!

Practical beliefs. This doctrine assures us that we can never be in any place where God is not present to hear our prayer and to receive our worship (Ps. 139:7-10). Nor are we ever physically or geographically beyond God's help for He is present whether we be in a prison (as Joseph, Gen. 39—40), or in a den of lions (as Daniel, Dan. 6), or in the emperor's presence (as Nehemiah, Neh. 2). According to Psalm 107 God is present to help when we are lost in the desert (vv. 4-9), in prisons (vv. 10-16), on a sick bed (vv. 17-22), or in storms at sea (vv. 24-30). The story of Jonah reminds us that our attempts to flee from God in disobedience are also futile.

A Problem: The doctrine, however, does raise a problem. How can an omnipresent God who dwells in heaven (Matt. 6:9, 1 Kings 8:30) come to earth? (Gen. 11:5) The Bible in most of these texts, is speaking of God's manifestation. He is manifest in a special way in heaven, so He is said to "dwell" there. He does also, as He chooses, specially manifest Himself on earth at various times and places, so we read that He comes to those places. Even the tabernacle in the wilderness and the first temple are said to be God's *mishkan,* dwelling (house). But His *shekinah,* dwelling (presence) was there also.

Omniscience of God

This term designates God's cognitive awareness. He has perfect, immediate, knowledge of all things, whether actual events or occurences conditioned by the acts of "free" beings. God knows all things past, present and future.

Scripture underscores God's perfect knowledge: "There is no creature hidden from His sight, but all things are open and laid bare to the eyes of Him with whom we have to do" (Heb. 4:13, NASB); "The eyes of the Lord run to and fro throughout the whole earth, to show Himself strong in the behalf of them whose heart is perfect toward Him" (2 Chron. 16:9). God requires no deductions or inductions of fact, no acquired knowledge. To Him, all things are eternal, present always in His mind.

Does God know conditional events of the future, even events dependent on the future acts of "free beings"? Some writers of theology deny this. "The knowledge of God," says Harold DeWolf, "must be limited by His own nature and purpose . . . if He has put a check on His power to give man freedom of will, then He must have limited somewhat His knowledge of the future . . . If God knows now every choice any man will ever make, then every choice is already determined and freedom is a delusion . . . if men have any margin of free will whatever, then God's foreknowledge of some of their choices must be a knowledge of probabilities, not of certainties" (DeWolf, *Theology*, p. 109).

But this seems contrary to the plain truth of the Scriptures. Old Testament prophecies of the career of Christ specify many details utterly conditional upon the future acts of yet unborn men. Predictive prophecy, of any meaningful sort, depends upon God's detailed foreknowledge. Precisely for this reason "modernist" or "liberal" writers quite uniformly deny the possibility of detailed predictions of the future in the Bible. But Peter says Christ was "delivered [crucified] by the determinate counsel and foreknowledge of God" (Acts 2:23).

The Bible suggests that even events men attribute to chance are under God's control (Prov. 16:33). Such knowledge is "wonderful" (Ps. 139:6), deep and incomprehensible (Rom. 11:33) to the truly devout. It is eminently wise (Ps. 104:24; Eph. 3:10). Free will and predestination present a great mystery, but true Christian piety should not deny what God reveals about them.

Omnipotence of God

Omnipotence means "all power." A biblical synonym is "Almighty" which is usually the translation of *Shaddai,* a name for God appearing often in the earliest parts of the Old Testament (see Ex. 6:3; Gen. 17:1; 35:11; 48:3). The theological doctrine is simply that God is able to do all things that are objects of power and that He is able to do so without diminution of His infinite strength.

We say that God is able to do all things that are "objects of power," since such things as the multiplication table, the law of noncontradiction, and other abstractions are not amenable or commensurate with power. Power has nothing to do with them.

Legislatures and kings neither originated them nor control them. So God's power must be understood in terms of the world He created, in harmony with His own reasonable nature.

Further, God exercises His power according to His own will. He never acts in power apart from wisdom. God is not the servant of His own unlimited energy. A scriptural way of saying this is, "He cannot deny Himself" (2 Tim. 2:13). Therefore, God "cannot be tempted with evil" (James 1:13) and He "cannot lie" (Titus 1:2).

Scriptural statements: Jesus said, "With God all things are possible" (Matt. 19:26). He meant to contrast God's ability with man's inability. Numerous other texts trace God's creative, sustaining, and governing power (Gen. 17:1; 18:18; Jer. 32:17; Job 42:1-2; Isa. 40:28; Eph. 1:11; Rev. 19:6).

Practical benefits: This doctrine assures us that "our God whom we serve is able" (Dan. 3:17). If we are sent as evangelists, He makes power available for results, as He pleases. "Who then can be saved? . . . with God all things are possible" (Matt. 19:25-26). If the course of the world seems perverse and threatening, God has power to change it—and power to judge and replace it with a better one. In due time, things will be "looking up" (Rev. 11:17; 19:6). God's omnipotence is a deep well of encouragement.

Incomprehensibility of God

This somewhat misleading term indicates simply that no one except the triune God fully comprehends God. Men should not find this difficult to accept, for we do not quite understand ourselves or our fellows. "The heart of kings is unsearchable" (Prov. 25:3). We do not fully understand because our minds are finite, whether operating in the sinlessness of Eden or in the presence of angels in heaven. Hence, we cannot, and never shall, fully understand all that an infinite God is and does.

Scriptural statements. Perhaps nothing will support this doctrine better than to place David's poetic statement alongside the magnificent expression of the Apostle Paul. Psalm 36:5-6 states, "Thy mercy, O Lord, is in the heavens; and Thy faithfulness reacheth unto the clouds. Thy righteousness is like the great mountains; Thy judgments are a great deep." Paul followed this with Romans 11:33, "O the depth of the riches both of the wisdom and knowledge of God! How unsearchable are His judgments, and His ways past finding out." God's mercy, faithfulness, righteousness, and His judgments, David wrote, in imaginative language, exceed human comprehension. Paul added to these God's wisdom, knowledge, and ways. Every aspect of the nature of our infinite God exceeds our limited comprehension (see also Job 5:9 and 11:7).

Practical benefits. Each of these texts represents a sensitive saint's worshipful wonder at the surpassing greatness of God. These things do not inspire long speeches; rather, they stimulate stumbling words of repentance and silence. Job is an excellent example (Job 42). They also lend support to two marvelous human impulses and enterprises—artistic expression and the pursuit of knowledge. No painter will ever exhaust the beauty of God's own workmanship; nor will an oratorio attain the heights and depths of the Lord whom the composer seeks to praise. As for learning, the researches of the learned disciplines, as one of Job's "friends" declared, will never reveal more than the outskirts of His ways. There will always be immensely more to challenge the greatest of human minds.

7

The Goodness of God

"O give thanks unto the Lord, for He is good" (Psalm 107:1).

The Book of Job opens by telling us that Job was a good man. He had a family of 10 children and immense wealth in livestock, and he "was the greatest of all men of the east" (Job 1:3, NASB).

Ownership of 7,000 sheep, 3,000 camels, 1,000 cattle, 500 female donkeys, and employment of hundreds of servants made Job great in men's eyes. What made him good? The fact that he was "blameless, upright, fearing God, and turning away from evil." This was goodness in God's eyes (Job 1:1, 8, NASB). Men who are great in wealth or intellectual power or fame may be small in character and wisdom. It is also possible for men to be little in fame, in goods, and physical power, and also be bad people. The true test is, what is a man in God's sight?

Sometimes, *good* means "perfection of character." So, when we say that a man is a good man, we intend to say that he has those traits of moral character that make him what a man ought to be. In this sense, the Bible says that God is holy, "of purer eyes than to behold evil" (Hab. 1:13).

On the other hand, we may be thinking of God's treatment of His creatures when we refer to His goodness: "God is good to Israel" (Ps. 73:1).

In this chapter, we are interested in the goodness of God in both these senses: what He is in His inward moral character, namely, *holy*, *true*, and *loving*; what He is in the manifestation of that moral character, namely, *righteous*, *faithful*, and *merciful*.

This type of analysis doesn't make most "modern" theologians very happy. Such headings and divisions are supposed to "lack religious value, and are contrary to the findings of modern psychology and religious experience. This judgment need not surprise us, for modern theology is in disagreement with the theological method of the old theologians who describe the divine attributes on the basis of, and according to, Scripture" (Francis Pieper, *Christian Dogmatics*, Concordia, 1950, I, 435). We hope to show, however, that this way of teaching men about the moral character of God and its manifestation among His creatures is according to the Bible.

No list of the divine attributes is fully satisfactory. We simply can't avoid overlapping and repetition. In so far as the terms are psychological in flavor, they lack the precision characteristic of language dealing with psychological analysis. Yet the human mind calls for "rhyme and reason in the relationship of qualities." So, if we are going to discuss features of moral character, God's or any other's, analysis is both helpful and necessary.

Holiness

God's moral character is holy. Biblical testimony to this fact is extensive: God's *person* is holy: "For the Lord our God is holy" (Ps. 99:9, see also vv. 1-8). God's *Spirit* is holy, "Take not Thy holy Spirit from me" (Ps. 51:11); God's *name* is holy, "Thus saith the high and lofty One that inhabiteth eternity, whose name is holy" (Isa. 57:15); God's *word* of promise is holy, "For He remembered His holy promise, and Abraham His servant" (Ps. 105:42). His *mighty acts* of power are deeds of holiness, "His right hand, and His holy arm, hath gotten Him the victory" (Ps. 98:1). God *swears* by His holiness, "Once have I sworn by My holiness" (Ps. 89:35). God's *habitation* in heaven (Deut. 26:15) and the *heavenly throne* from which He reigns (Ps. 47:8), as well as His *temple* at Jerusalem (Hab. 2:20), and *objects* there devoted to Him (Lev. 27:28;

Zech. 14:20-21) are holy. Such texts could be multiplied indefinitely.

What does *holy* mean? Our English word is related to *hale* and *whole*, that is, "in one piece, sound, healthy." The common meanings are (1) belonging to or coming from God, (2) untainted by evil or sin, (3) deserving of reverence (R. Flesch and A. H. Lass, editors. *Webster's New World Dictionary of the American Language.* New York: Popular Library, Inc.). This group of ideas is essentially what we find in the Bible.

Biblical usage indicates various meanings for the word *holy*. Whatever is set apart by men for special purposes is holy. Such a nonreligious use is roughly equivalent to *dedicated*. Anything set apart from common use and devoted entirely to God is holy. And something separated from evil of any sort is holy. This meaning, the sense of moral purity, is why *holy* (suggesting hale, whole, or sound) was used by early translators of the Bible into English for this central feature of God's character. To be less than holy is not only to be unsound (unhealthy or less than whole), but also unclean, defiled, or corrupt.

God is holy in that He exists on a level of being entirely apart from all that is creaturely, earthly, or human: "The Lord reigneth; let the people tremble; He sitteth between the cherubims; let the earth be moved. The Lord is great in Zion; and He is high above all the people. Let them praise Thy great and terrible name; for it is holy . . . worship at His footstool; for He is holy" (Ps. 99:1-3, 5b). He is "the high and lofty One that inhabiteth eternity, whose name is Holy; I dwell in the high and holy place" (Isa. 57:15).

If God is the high, lofty One, above all people, as these Scripture texts say, He is also far removed from all that is sinful. In the Bible, especially the prophets, holiness as moral purity becomes the most prevalent and important affirmation God makes about Himself. And in the New Testament, God's moral purity is almost the exclusive sense of His holiness.

Both ideas—God's transcendence as Creator and His purity as moral Governor—appear together frequently in Scripture. For example, in his beatific vision, Isaiah first saw the Lord, "high and lifted up . . . holy, holy holy" (Isa. 6:1-4). But the vision immediately made the prophet aware, not so much of his creatureliness as of his sinfulness (vv. 5-7). So, later, when Isaiah reported God's lofty residence in heaven, the prophet added that God hates all that is morally impure (Isa. 57:15-17).

In the language of worship, we find the same two ideas, God's distance from us as Creator and His moral purity: "Who shall ascend into the hill of the Lord? or who shall stand in His holy place? He that hath clean hands, and a pure heart; who hath not lifted up his soul unto vanity, nor sworn deceitfully" (Ps. 24:3-4).

Since God's holiness is the fundamental attribute of His moral character, we may be certain that the appearance that wickedness prospers more than righteousness is misleading. It is better to do right because we know that the holy God, our Creator, is our Governor and "will judge the world in righteousness by that Man whom He hath ordained" (Acts 17:31). Though man's conscience tells him nothing of God's love and mercy, it assures him of God's holiness.

> Careless seems the great Avenger;
>   history's pages but record
> One death—grapple in the darkness
>   'twixt old systems and the Word;
> Truth forever on the scaffold,
>   wrong forever on the throne,—
> Yet that scaffold sways the future,
>   and behind the dim unknown,
> Standeth God within the shadow,
> keeping watch above His own.
>
> (James Russell Lowell, *The Present Crisis*)

The practical importance of God's holiness extends to many aspects of the Christian life and hope for the future. As we have noted, God's holiness exposes our sin and our need for cleansing as well as forgiveness (Isa. 6:1, 5). His holiness assures us that God will not renege on anything He has said, neither warning nor promise. "My covenant will I not break . . . Once have I sworn by My holiness . . . I will not lie" (Ps. 89:34-35). The sphere of salvation will always be one of orderly morality, for His "holy arm" brings it to pass (Ps. 98:1) and with righteousness He reigns (vv. 2-9). His invisible kingdom now and His manifest kingdom of the future are also holy (Ps. 47:8; Isa. 11). Finally, God's holiness both demands and provides the holiness of His people: "For I am the Lord your God: ye shall therefore sanctify yourselves, and ye shall be holy; for I am holy" (Lev. 11:44; see 1 Peter 1:15-16; Heb. 12:10).

Righteousness

Since God is holy in character every manifestation of that character is righteous. The Bible therefore speaks frequently of the righteousness of God.

We may think of God's righteousness in three ways. First, God always acts in harmony with His own holy nature. He loves righteousness (Ps. 11:7), so He cannot lie (Titus 1:2); He will never deny Himself (2 Tim. 2:13) nor fail to keep His covenant promises. If He saves a sinner, it will be in a way consistent with His own holy nature. If He establishes a moral law, it will be righteous, precisely because it will be an expression of His holy will.

Since God is sovereign, He does not have to answer the question, Why? And we have no right to ask. His laws are right because they express His holiness. God's laws are expressions of a moral will which in turn is an expression of a holy character. The righteousness by which God orders His world is neither something created, external to Himself, nor something other than God himself. His righteous acts are His character in action; God is law unto Himself.

Second, God deals with His creatures in justice (righteous treatment). The classical theologians call this *rectoral* justice when viewed as administration of His universal government. "Righteousness and justice are the foundation of Thy throne" (Ps. 89:14, NASB). It is called *distributive* justice when it involves giving each of His creatures his due reward or punishment, "Righteous art Thou, O Lord, and upright are Thy judgments" (Ps. 119:137). It is called *punitive* or vindicatory (not vindictive) justice when it is in connection with punishment of sin because of sin's intrinsic ill-desert, for the scepter of God's kingdom is a scepter of equity (see Ps. 45:3-7).

Third, we must think of God's righteousness as the imputed righteousness of God. First mentioned in Genesis 15:6 in connection with Abraham's faith, this is the righteousness received in justification. Christ's righteousness becomes vicariously ours, imparted to us by God when we believe on His Son. The amazing doctrine is taught throughout the Scriptures (see Rom. 3:21) but treated at length by Paul (Rom. 3:21—5:21; Gal. 1—4). This is not God's attribute, even though the fact that God declares ungodly sinners, who are not righteous, to be righteous, must be squared with God's truthfulness and justice. God is both "just, and the justifier of him which believeth in Jesus" (Rom. 3:26).

God's righteousness will be manifest at last on the Judgment Day (Rev. 16:4-7) just as, long ago, it was manifest when it pleased the Lord to bruise His Son at Calvary, when He took our place as sinners (Isa. 53:10; Rom. 3:25). If we are wise, we will see God's righteousness in His treatment of us as believers, not only in forgiving our sins (1 John 1:9) but in chastening us (Dan. 9:14) and demanding a righteous life from us. If we have difficulty at times seeing God's justice in the way He temporarily allows evil to prosper, we may nevertheless trust His justice to triumph at last (Jer. 12:1-4).

> Though the cause of Evil prosper,
>   yet 'tis Truth alone is strong,
> And, albeit, she wander outcast now.
>   I see around her throng
> Troops of beautiful, tall angels,
>   to enshield her from all wrong.
>
> (James Russell Lowell, *The Present Crisis*)

Truth

It will help us to understand this attribute of the Godhead to quote several leading statements of Scripture before we give a definition. Jesus prayed to His Father as "the only true God" (John 17:3) and

Paul spoke of Christian conversion as a turning "to God from idols to serve the living and true God" (1 Thes. 1:9).

In these passages, *true* means "genuine, the real, the valid." In contrast to idols, demonic spirits and all false objects of veneration, God is genuine God: "We know that an idol is nothing in the world and that there is none other God but one . . . though there be that are called gods" (1 Cor. 8:4-5). Of all the alleged objects of discourse called god, the God of the Bible is the only true God. He is *veritable* God. God's attributes and actions are true. God's peace, for example, is true peace (Jer. 33:6); likewise His kindness is true kindness (2 Sam. 2:6); His goodness, true goodness (Ex. 34:6); and His grace, true grace (John 1:17).

He is also the *veracious*, truth-speaking, truth-communicating God: "Let God be [found] true, but every man a liar" (Rom. 3:4); "I will . . . praise Thy name for Thy lovingkindness and for Thy truth: for Thou hast magnified Thy word above all Thy name (Ps. 138:2; see also John 3:33; Rom. 1:25; John 14:17; 1 John 5:7).

Since the veritable (true) and veracious (truthful) God is the Creator and Governor of heaven and earth, a third sense appears: He is the ground of all truth. Scripture thus addresses Him as "Lord God of truth" (Ps. 31:5).

Christians, therefore, should be neither cynics nor skeptics. The cynical temper, doubting everything and everybody, challenging every statement as if there were no true statements, has only the appearance of the love of truth. We know that God is truthful, that He made our organs of sense and powers of reason not to mock us but to bring us into cognitive touch with a universe that is genuine. Skeptics and cynics are out of touch with God's world.

This is asserted directly in passages such as Psalm 111, which discuss God's works. The works of God are first said to be great, honorable, and wonderful. Then, "the works of His hands are verity and judgment; all His commandments are sure. They stand fast for ever and ever, and are done in truth and uprightness" (Ps. 111:7-8).

Christians, as lovers of God, are lovers of all truth because we know Him that is true (John 8:13-14, 16, 18, 28). Our God is the

Author of truth. His children, therefore, should not be obscurantists. They will be lovers of true chemistry and astronomy, as well as of true Christian doctrine and true Bible interpretation.

Faithfulness

Since God is true, He will not change His character. He will be true to Himself. To us, His creatures, He will remain the same as He has always been.

A number of important texts declare this truth, but Deuteronomy 7:9-11 is outstanding: "Know therefore that the Lord thy God, He is God, the faithful God, which keepeth covenant and mercy with them that love Him and keep His commandments to a thousand generations; and repayeth them that hate Him to their face, to destroy them: He will not be slack to him that hateth Him, He will repay him to his face. Thou shalt therefore keep the commandments, and the statutes, and the judgments, which I command thee this day to do them." In keeping with this trait, He is called a Rock (Deut. 32:4, 15, 18; Ps. 19:14), a Fortress (Jer. 16:19), a Defense (Ps. 89:18); His Word is said to be sure (Ps. 19:7) and steadfast forever (Dan. 6:26).

When hoary time shall pass away,
    and earthly thrones and kingdoms fall;
When men who here refuse to pray,
    On rocks and hills and mountains call;
God's love, so sure, shall still endure,
    All measureless and strong;
Redeeming grace to Adam's race—
    The saints' and angels' song.

                        Frederick M. Lehman

Because God is steadfast, the world of nature, the sphere of His creation, preservation, and providence will remain steadfast, "While the earth remaineth, seedtime and harvest, and cold and heat, and summer and winter, and day and night shall not cease" (Gen. 8:22). The farmer may plant his crops knowing that within the variety of climate and rainfall he can count on a crop if he tends his fields. The scientist may count on what he calls the uniformity of nature. Gravity, the rates of expansion of gases, the velocities of electrons and light waves will be everywhere the same. Natural events can be explained by natural causes. Superstitions, "old wives' fables," and astrology may be ignored. God's faithfulness is the solid foundation of reality, and the life of intelligent action.

In the spiritual realm, God's promises are trustworthy; His covenants are unbreakable. Ethan the Ezrahite sang of this in Psalm 89: "With my mouth will I make known Thy faithfulness to all generations . . . Thy faithfulness shalt Thou establish in the very heavens" (vv. 1-2). He said the heavens as well as the congregation of believers on earth shall praise God's faithfulness (v. 5). God is faithful in His rule of nature (vv. 9-13). But His faithfulness was singularly prominent in His dealings with the house of David, defending the anointed sons when they kept the covenant, faithfully chastening them for their own good when they did not (vv. 20-32). David's seed, the Psalm says, "shall endure forever," a promise pointing to the endless resurrection life of our Lord Jesus Christ, "as a faithful witness in heaven" (vv. 36-37).

This truth has an obverse side too. If God will fulfill His promises faithfully, He will also carry out His threats. This is part of "He cannot deny Himself" (2 Tim. 2:13). "Be not deceived; God is not mocked; for whatsoever a man soweth, that shall he also reap" (Gal. 6:7).

Great is Thy faithfulness, O God my Father,
There is no shadow of turning with Thee;
Thou changest not, Thy compassions they fail not;
As Thou hast been Thou for ever wilt be.
Thomas O. Chisholm

Love

Another of God's attributes of goodness is love. We must make a distinction here between love and mercy. We regard mercy as a manifestation of love, just as faithfulness is a manifestation of His truth, and righteousness of His holiness.

Love is exceedingly difficult to mention, in times like ours, without the danger of misinterpretation. Physical passion, the mutual attraction of the sexes, seems to be such an absorbing interest of our times that this form of attraction tends to monopolize our thinking about love.

The distinctive element in the love of God is self-communication. This must be distinguished from either holiness or truth. It certainly does not include them. If we confuse these three in any way whatsoever, we create serious problems. If we equate holiness and love, we may easily overlook sin, for then holiness is no barrier. Justice is made maudlin. Hell and final judgment are then unnecessary. If we equate love and truth, then we may overlook falsehood. True, "God is love," (1 John 4:8), but this means that God is a loving Being, just as He is also holy and true.

As anyone should know who has read the stories of God's chastening of the Israelites (Exodus to Malachi), God's love for them was at every point directed and limited by His holiness. There is nothing maudlin about the love of God.

God spared not His own Son, therefore, when His Son became sin for us at Calvary (2 Cor. 5:21), God caused Him to be "wounded for our transgressions . . . It pleased the Lord to bruise Him" (Isa. 53:5, 10). Thus, we see in what poignant ways holiness and love meet, "for God so loved the world that He gave His only begotten Son" (John 3:16).

A well-known hymn says that God's "love found a way to redeem my soul! Love found a way that could make me whole." And, indeed, God's love did. But not at the expense of His truth and holiness. The "expense" was the life of His only begotten Son.

Neither is God's love a mere "positive attitude." Quite to the contrary, He hates not only "wickedness" (Ps. 45:7), but also "all workers of iniquity" (Ps. 5:5).

God's love is first of all holy. It is incorrect to say that God's love is unconditional, for it is conditioned by His holiness and His love of Himself—namely, by truth. He did not need a world to have an object of love. God loves the world of men because they bear His image. His love is *holy,* designed fully to restore that image but also *true* in that our sinfulness is taken into account.

If God was to love us sinners, then He had to count the cost of that love. Salvation through the passion and death of the Son of God was the fruit of that suffering love, for Christ is "the Lamb slain from the foundation of the world" (Rev. 13:8; 1 Peter 1:19-20).

The Bible makes God's love not only the ground of proper human love (1 John 4:11), but also the effective cause of it, for "we love Him, because He first loved us" (1 John 4:19). Love is the evidence and fruit of God's indwelling presence in us and the means God uses to reveal His holiness and love to the world (1 John 4:12).

Mercy

Mercy is often called *transitive love,* and such it is. It is love in action for those who do not deserve the provisions of God's love but who desperately need it.

The country music star, Eddie Arnold, sings a song about a lover who reflects sadly that the great love of his life, one who married another, never knew he loved her because he never told her!

This is not true of God's love, for His mercies on the undeserving have been showered upon them. He has shown it in His care for all His creatures (Ps. 145:15-16), and especially in His forbearance of His enemies and blasphemers (Neh. 9:17-21; 27-32). A psalmist exclaimed that "the earth, O Lord, is full of Thy mercy" (Ps. 119:64).

The goodness (benevolence) of God toward all His creatures, especially sinful men, is a special feature of God's mercy. Paul declared that God's goodness is a witness even among the heathen (Acts 14:17). Joined with holiness, truth, and love, God's kindness has a special appeal to sinful men, "Despisest thou the riches of His goodness and forbearance and long-suffering; not knowing that the goodness of God leadeth thee to repentance?" (Rom. 2:4)

The Triunity of the Godhead

"The name of the Father, and of the Son, and of the Holy Ghost" (Matt. 28:19).

In A.D. 325 there assembled at Nicea, a city of Asia Minor not far from Constantinople, 318 fathers (bishops, or pastors) from churches throughout the Roman world. Their purpose was to formulate a written statement of biblical teaching about the relation of the Father, the Son, and the Holy Spirit in the Godhead.

What Christians now call the doctrine of the Holy Trinity is latent in the Bible and it had been a part of Christian baptism and worship from earliest Christian times. The council at Nicea was the first common effort to define the doctrine against the errors of several divisive teachers and sects which were challenging a foundational Christian truth. The Nicean fathers never conceived of their effort as one to dissolve the essential mystery of the teaching; they recognized that such a thing could not be done. Nor were they attempting to frame a "metaphysical" definition of God. What they wanted to do was state in some intelligible way the fact that Father, Son, and Holy Spirit are three, without denying in any fashion that God is one Lord.

The result of their labor was a statement of belief affirming that the oneness of the Godhead is in being (Latin *substantia*, substance; Greek *ousia*). The Son is *homoousios* (the same substance) with the Father. And the Spirit is to be worshiped together with the Father and Son.

About a century later (A.D. 451) at a place called Chalcedon not far from Nicea, the Latin words *persona* (mask) and the Greek word *hypostasis* (in the English New Testament, "person," Gal. 2:6; "substance," Heb. 11:1) were adopted as designations for the sense in which the Members of the Trinity are three. These early Christians made no effort to phrase the biblical revelation in the thought pattern of Greek philosophy. The contrary was the case. The simple doctrines of Scripture—the Father is God; the Son is God; the Holy Spirit is God; yet there is only one God—were preserved in resistance to the efforts of some teachers to dissolve the mystery of God's nature in some philosophic formula. The confessions of Nicea and Chalcedon are with us to this day as standards because they leave the mysteries of Scriptures intact.

You may wonder if such technicalities are necessary. Yes, if you are going to meet the challenges to the deity of our Lord which are mounting in our time, just as they were prior to the Nicean Council. Arius, a pastor from Alexandria, advocated the very same reasonable-sounding, fatal denials that we hear from learned "modernists" and the unlearned cultists today. He wanted to worship Christ as a kind of great angel, the first created being. Another minister at Alexandria, Athanasius, insisted, on scriptural grounds, that Christ is no created being. Like the Father, He is an eternal Being, consubstantial ("the same substance," Greek *homoousios*) with the Father. The difference may be small but it involves the very heartbeat of our faith, the full deity of Jesus.

Four hundred years ago Arianism (Socinianism or Unitarianism) again challenged the orthodox faith. The great Reformers responded valiantly and successfully. Without mentioning the names of the contemporary sixteenth-century Arians, John Calvin insisted that Christian people of all ages must reject the teaching that makes Christ less than God and in doing so must also learn a few strange, new words. Calvin pointed out that for ages saintly people (Hilary, Jerome, Augustine) protested the use of these words but nevertheless had to employ them. Then he wisely added,

"And this modesty of saintly men ought to warn us against forthwith . . . taking to task those who do not wish to swear by the words conceived by us." Thus he sympathized with the simple man's impatience with unfamiliar words. But he went on to insist that the simple man too, must have some patience.

Without precise terms, said Calvin, we cannot clarify issues and distinguish a teacher who is a willful, dangerous heretic from one who is mildly erroneous or entirely orthodox. "Arius says that Christ is God, but mutters that He was made and had a beginning. He says that Christ is one with the Father, but secretly whispers in the ears of his own partisans that He is united to the Father like other believers, although by a singular privilege. Say 'consubstantial' and you will tear off the mask of this turncoat, and yet you add nothing to Scripture" (*Institutes,* I, xii, 5).

Why Christians Believe in the Trinity

Why do Christians everywhere insist on this doctrine? No text of Scripture says specifically that God eternally exists as one Being (*sustantia* substance,) in three Persons, each of which fully and perfectly possesses that substance. The orthodox doctrine is that each of the Members is God in a *quantitative* sense—all the God there is—not in any mere *generic* sense as when we say all men are human, as a class or category of being. Christians insist that this is necessary to believe. Again, why?

The answer has to do with history, not church history, but biblical history. The Old Testament tells how God called Abram out of a culture where many gods were worshiped (Josh. 24:2) in order to make known to him the sole existence of the one, true God. The Lord used Abram to create a people through whom that message could be conveyed to other families of earth and He established the truth of monotheism within the descendents of Abram at the time of Moses. The Old Testament historical books tell of the frequent apostasies of the Israelites from this belief and of their permanent acceptance of it through the sufferings of the Babylonian exile. After that, Israel's apostasies from monotheism were never repeated on a general scale.

The first disciples of Jesus were Jews (Israelites). As time passed these incurable monotheists recognized that Jesus of Nazareth was God, the same God their fathers had worshipped under Moses. They said so in their sermons and writings.

Before He died, Jesus told them that the Father would send to them another Comforter, the Spirit of truth, to "abide . . . forever." He was to be another (*allos*) of the same, not a different (*heteros*) kind. When He, the Holy Spirit, came in the special way, described in the second chapter of Acts, the disciples immediately recognized Him also as God. They formed no doctrinal statement, but while steadfastly acknowledging that there is only one God (as all Jews affirmed), they also affirmed that the Father is God, the Son is God, and the Spirit is God. They prayed *in* the Spirit *to* the Father *in the name of* the Son. In their benedictions they pronounced the grace of our Lord Jesus Christ and the love of God the Father and the communion of the Holy Spirit on their departing assemblies (2 Cor. 13:14). Baptism, by the Lord's command, was in the name of the Father and of the Son and of the Holy Ghost (Matt. 28:19).

Every element mentioned in this last paragraph is woven into the fabric of the New Testament. The combination of the elements was bound to come. Significantly, the earliest, post-New Testament Christian creed is essentially a confession of faith in "God the Father Almighty . . . and in Jesus Christ, His only Son . . . and in the Holy Ghost (the "Old Roman Creed," found in H. Bettenson, *Documents of the Christian Church,* Oxford, 1947, p. 33).

The Church today is by no means bound blindly to follow ancient traditions. Yet, we may thank God for what previous generations of devout Christian scholars and teachers have done to formulate the doctrines of Christianity. This is the true apostolic succession, guarding a deposit, or committing to a rising generation of believers what has been passed down (2 Tim. 2:1-2).

Old Testament Preparation

The Old Testament prepared for revelation of the triunity of the Godhead by raising questions and posing problems which suggest the New Testament revelation. The most common name for God (*'elohim*), appearing in the first sentence in the Bible, is a plural form. The sense, however, is almost always singular, when used of the God of the Bible. Once, however, (Gen. 35:7) the Hebrew would normally be translated, apart from the context, "the gods were revealed to him," even though the one true God is meant. Also, several times God refers to Himself as "Us" (Gen. 1:26; 3:22; 11:7; Isa. 6:8) and there are contexts in which God, in a puzzling way, seems to be more than one Person (see Gen. 18:2, 16; 19:2; Isa. 44:6). Psalm 110:1 is a special case, because Jesus commented on the verse to prove that it is not improper for men to call Him the Son of God (Matt. 22:41-46). None of these passages clearly teaches a plurality of persons in the Godhead, but it is not inappropriate (as Jesus' use of one of them shows) to challenge teachers who reject the Trinity to provide a better explanation of the verses.

A startlingly impressive passage in Isaiah (63:7-10) brings the Lord [Jehovah], "the angel of His presence" and "His holy Spirit" together. And in another passage, we read, "there am I: and now the Lord God and His Spirit hath sent me" (Isa. 48:16). If the one who refers to himself as "I" and "me" is the Servant of Isaiah (52:12—53:12) then this text does indeed have a trinitarian ring.

None of these Old Testament passages is sufficient ground for a doctrine of three Persons in the Godhead. No Jew was looking for the God-Man at Bethlehem, so far as we know, on the basis of any of these or similar passages. Yet the revelation of the Trinity furnished a basis for understanding these texts of the Old Testament.

The New Testament Doctrine

The North Star of all biblical teaching is the unity of God. Our Lord commented favorably on the Mosaic formula, "The Lord our God is one Lord" (Deut. 6:4; Mark 12:28-29) and His disciples, reared in Judaism, never doubted it. They would never have followed a Messiah who announced a doctrine of tritheism (three gods) and neither they nor their Lord ever entertained such a repugnant, pagan thought.

As we have seen, the idea of three Members in the one Godhead was thrust upon the first Christians by events of salvation history. The New Testament, we should note, was written after the deity of the Lord Jesus Christ and the "Other Comforter" had been thoroughly accepted. Thus, numerous expressions occur in its pages which can be interpreted as referring to *persons* recognized by the early believers as God. The three persons are "God the Father," "Christ . . . who is over all, God" and "the Holy Ghost . . . God" (see John 6:27; Rom. 9:5; Acts 5:3-4). Of these Persons there are three, no more, no less.

The distinction between the three Members can be demonstrated in several lengthy passages, Ephesians 1:3-14, for example. It is particularly apparent in John 14 where all three divine Persons are mentioned by Jesus Himself in distinct ways. Speaking to the Twelve Apostles after Judas' departure from the Upper Room, our Lord said, "I will pray the Father, and He shall give you another Comforter" (v. 16). Then, after discussing the Spirit's coming and future relationship to believers, Jesus added, "But the Comforter, which is the Holy Ghost, . . . the Father will send in My name" (v. 26).

The baptism of Jesus reveals a similar clear distinction between the Persons (Luke 3:21-22; John 1:32-34; Matt. 3:16-17; Mark 1:9-11). We do not know how many people were present, but John the Baptizer was there and reported what he did, what he saw, and what he heard (John 1:32-34). Jesus came to the Jordan River where John was baptizing. The two men entered the water and John baptized Jesus. John saw the Spirit descending in the form of a dove and the voice of the Father was heard saying, "This is My beloved Son, in whom I am well pleased" (Matt. 3:17).

The essential, substantial unity of the Godhead is also preserved in the New Testament. There is only one God, not three gods. John 14:23, for example, states that when believers love Christ and keep His words, the Son and the Father come in the Spirit. Some statements affirm the unity in even more specific language. The indwelling of "the Spirit of God," Paul wrote, is the indwelling of "the Spirit of Christ" (Rom. 8:9; John 14:18). The argument of 1 Corinthians 3:16 draws a parallel between the indwelling of the Spirit in the church and the indwelling of the Old Testament temple by the God of the Old Testament, namely, Jehovah. Finally in John 10:30 Jesus said, "I and My Father are one."

There is no regular order of the names of the three divine persons. Because of our familiarity with the order of the three designations in the Great Commission and baptismal formula of Matthew 28:19 we naturally think of the three as Father, Son, and Holy Spirit, in that order. But in the familiar benediction of 2 Corinthians 13:14, the order is Christ, God (Father), Spirit. In Ephesians 4:4-6 the order is Spirit, Lord (Christ), Father. (See also 1 Cor. 12:4-6, Jude 20-21; Eph. 5:18-20; 2 Thes. 2:13-14.)

Nor do the relationships indicated by "Son of" and "Spirit of" indicate inferiority. The Son has the same *power* that the Father has, "For as the Father raiseth up the dead, and quickeneth them, even so the Son quicketh whom He will" (John 5:21). He also deserves the same honor: "that all men should honor the Son, even as they honor the Father" (John 5:23).

The New Testament does indicate, however, a certain priority and subordination among the Persons. This has reference to the work of the three Members and their respective functional relationships, not to their being.

Regretfully, some famous and influential theologians of our time apparently affirm the triune God but explain their doctrine in ways which deny the distinctness of the three persons. They may endorse ancient creeds, but according to their own claims their "recitals" are "doxological"—a mode of religious confession without actually intending exactly what one says. They deny the doctrine of "one substance-three persons" in favor of one substance, one person, three modes of working.

We must not be so cautious, however, that while affirming the *sameness of what the persons are* we fail to distinguish the *differences* of *who they are* and *what they do* within the Holy Trinity.

Certain texts of the New Testament seem to provide a formula for at least a glimpse of the relations, functional and external, of the three Persons. In explaining the meaningless vanity of idols Paul wrote, "Yet for us there is but one God, the Father, from [*ek*, out of] whom are all things, and we exist for Him, and one Lord, Jesus Christ, through whom are all things, and we exist through Him" (1 Cor. 8:6, NASB). The passage has the ring of a familiar formula of some kind. There is no mention of the Holy Spirit, but Paul completed the ideas when he elsewhere wrote, "Through Him [Christ] we . . . have our access in one Spirit to [*pros*, to toward] the Father" (Eph. 2:18, NASB). This suggests that the Father is the source in creation and redemption, the *planner*; the Son is the channel or means, the *mediator*; the Spirit is agent, the *applier*.

An examination of the doctrine of the triune God, in Ephesians 1, yields similar results in the analysis of the work of the Trinity in redemption. Here the Father, the One who planned redemption, is said to have *chosen* us (vv. 3-6); Christ the Son *provides* our redemption (vv. 7-13a); the Spirit is the seal and earnest of fully *applied* redemption (vv. 13b-14).

We are also taught by New Testament examples to pray *to* the Father, *in* the Spirit, *in the name of* Jesus, the Son. This shows that, in our approach to the Godhead in worship and prayer, the functions of the three Members are to be acknowledged.

Illustrations

Illustrations of the Trinity, however helpful, are inevitably dangerous, for if carried beyond a very narrow area of the subject, they introduce denials of what must necessarily always remain a mystery. God cannot, of course, be one and three in the same sense. This is not the hard part. How can each person possess the whole being-essence-substance without dividing it? That is the difficulty.

A friend of mine examined St. Augustine's illustrations in *de Trinitate* (*On the Trinity*) and thought he found 13 of them, all psychological, resting on the fact of man's bearing the image of God. Augustine traced correspondences between the Holy Trinity and trinities of various sorts in man's rational and mental make-up. His best one is the power of the soul to dialogue with itself. *I* ponder *me* when I inwardly reflect on any question; then objectively, in a kind of third capacity—the *neutral spectator*—I render a decision. This is a "safe" illustration but the yield of understanding is small.

A favorite since the Middle Ages is water [one *substance*], present somewhere on earth in purity but in three *forms* at all times, that is to say, it exists in three *modes*: liquid, solid (ice), gas (vapor). This one, which seems to clarify everything, quickly leads to denial of any Trinity at all in favor of Sabellian modalism.

Nature pretty well fails to provide an illustration of the Trinity which does not also lead to error if followed seriously. Two diagrams have been widely accepted. The equilateral triangle, each side equal (Father, Son, Holy Spirit), each "containing" the tri-

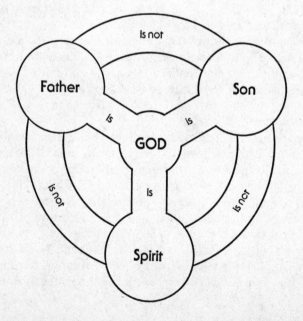

angle (God) is as good as any common figure. But do the sides each contain the whole? The "Shield of the Trinity" is the best diagram so far proposed. The ancient form of it, in which the writing is all in Latin, is here translated. It merits study.

There are many other illustrations. The inadequacies and dangers in them all underscore the essential, necessary, ineluctable mystery of the Trinity. It is a revelation. Like all revelations of God we know it is true, because God has told us about it; we carry rational understanding as far as our powers of thought and limitations of information take us, but, ultimately, we must stop in the presence of inscrutable mystery.

Questions about the Doctrine

How shall we interpret certain puzzling statements in the Bible about the Persons of the Triune God?

1. Why, if the Second Person is equal and coeternal with the Father, is He very frequently called the *Son of God*? This seems to many Christian people, especially new believers, to indicate that the Son had a beginning in time. It seems to say the Son is derived somehow from the Father. On the contrary, in Hebrew usage, "son of" is often used metaphorically to indicate something about the character or condition of a person rather than His origin. Thus, a literal rendering of Genesis 7:6 says, "Noah was a son of six hundred years," that is, six hundred years old. Similarly, James and John were "sons of Thunder," that is, forceful in speech. The people of Jesus' time understood *Son of God* to mean a divine person, not the offspring of God. So when Jesus accepted the accolade, the Jews took up stones to stone Him for blasphemy (John 5:18), since they rejected His claim. *Son of God* simply means "divine person, a person who is God."

2. What does *only begotten* mean when used of Christ's relation to the Father? (John 3:16, 18; 1:14; 1:18; 1 John 4:9) *Only begotten* is a favorite expression of John. The English expression appears to be related to the word *beget*, the function of a male parent in the conception of a child. The Greek word also is similar in form to the word *to beget*. Scholars have firmly established, however,

that the Greek word *mono-gen-es* (only begotten) is not directly related to the word *genna-o*, to beget, but to *gen-es*, family, kind or class. *Monogenes*, the word translated *only begotten*, means "only-one-of-its-kind." So in John 3:16, and the other texts cited above, "only," or "unique" is the true sense.

3. In what sense is Christ the *Firstborn* in Romans 8:29 and Hebrews 1:6? Again, Jewish custom and word usage supply the adequate answer. The first male child was normally the heir. He had preeminent position and rights of primogeniture in the family. So Christ is, of all God's creation, the One having preeminence. The term has nothing to say about the time of His origin.

Two Traditional Expressions

Two expressions have been traditionally employed to designate certain inner relations between the Father and the Son, and the Father and Son with the Spirit. These two expressions are the *eternal generation* of the Son by the Father and the *eternal spiration* (or procession) of the Spirit from the Father and the Son. They began to be employed about the time of the Council of Nicea (A.D. 325). They expressed in scriptural language the idea that the Son and the Spirit were eternally with the Godhead. John 1:14 refers to our Lord as the "only Begotten" of the Father. And John 14:16, 26 and 15:26 speak of the Spirit as "proceeding" from the Father and the Son.

Says the noted Lutheran Church-Missouri Synod theologian, Francis Pieper, these internal works "are not common to all three Persons . . . but are ascribed to one or two Persons. The generation of the Son is ascribed only to the Father, the spiration of the Holy Ghost only to the Father and the Son, and thereby the Father is revealed as a person distinct from the Son and the Holy Spirit as distinct from the Father and the Son." Pieper adds: "This terminology is not meaningless jargon, but necessary theological apparatus. Of course, Christians might wish that the Church would never have been troubled by Unitarians and therefore would have had no occasion to formulate this terminology [He mentions several very technical Latin terms]. Christians say with St. Paul: 'I would they were even cut off which trouble you' (Gal. 5:12). But . . . this terminology became necessary on account of the errors and the treachery of the heretics" (*Christian Dogmatics*, I, 416-417).

The intransigence of orthodox people on their teaching seems strange in our extremely accommodating, compromising, and undogmatic times. If it seems excessive, or if the language of the creeds and confessions seem unnecessarily harsh in condemnation, we should recall the words of the Apostles: "Whosoever denieth the Son, the same hath not the Father" (1 John 2:23); "Every spirit that does not confess Jesus is not from God; and this is the spirit of the antichrist" (1 John 4:3, NASB); "If any man love not the Lord Jesus Christ, let him be anathema" (1 Cor. 16:22).

Values of the Doctrine

The Triunity of God suggests an answer to the ancient question, What was God doing before He created the world? He was not preparing hell for the overcurious, as one facetious wag in Augustine's time suggested, but was engaged in loving, interpersonal fellowship within the Godhead.

It would be impossible for our minds to grasp all the facts centering in the atoning work of Christ, except in terms of the Triune Godhead. "For God [the Father] so loved the world that He gave His only begotten Son, that whosoever believeth in Him [through the conviction and enabling of the Holy Spirit] should not perish" (John 3:16).

In an age of social emphasis in all realms of learning and action, a triad of Persons rather than a monad gives greater appeal to the Christian faith.

The value, however, cannot really be estimated. Christianity is in every way a Trinitarian faith.

God's Eternal Plan
for the Heavens and the Earth

He "worketh all things after the counsel of His own will" (Eph. 1:11).

With the help of several scientific instruments, we know that there are small fluctuations in the amount of energy released by the sun. We also know that the amount of that energy reaching us on Planet Earth varies with the seasons. To judge by what the human eyes can see, however, the sun is immutable. It remains forever constant, steady, *faithful*.

When the earth tilts the northern pole of its axis away from the sun, as it does between September 21 and March 21, that polar area loses heat, subsides into winter and only gradually recovers warmth as it tilts back toward the sun. The sun is steady; the earth is the variable.

In a similar way God is immutable—that is, He does not change. Another name for this is *faithfulness*. Yet when we think about God's relation with variable men and a changing world, it is hard for us to maintain this vision of God. So Scripture speaks of God in a two-fold manner: (1) In His majesty existing above time and space (Ps. 90:4, "A thousand years in Thy sight are but as yesterday"). (2) In accordance with our human views as entering time and space. Only in this second sense is God comprehensible to us.

A modern, conservative Lutheran theologian makes the distinction this way: "We must so think of God that [He] . . . who in

His being is immutable, is angry or merciful according to the difference in the object of His affection. We must so conceive of God that in spite of the immutability of His essence He is a gracious God to the humble, poor, and contrite sinners, but a jealous God to the proud and self-righteous (1 Peter 5:5; Luke 1:52-53; 18:9-14). God remains immutable, but there is mutability [changeableness] in the object of His affection." The way God *is* and the way we must apprehend Him are two different things (F. Pieper, *Christian Dogmatics*, I, 441-442).

Another old illustration also involves the sun. A blob of wax on a varnished table by a south window, placed there at nightfall, will remain rigid all night. But the nature of wax is such that come late morning, when the changeless sun shines through the window on it, the changeable wax warms up, melts, and runs away.

The faithfulness (immutability) of God has some important bearing on the way men think about life. We should always hold in mind that we only partially understand the subject, that is, just as much as God has revealed. We men are aware that we have a certain freedom to think and act the way we please. Yet, we learn early that there are limits. We meet restrictions in rules, laws, other persons and the limited powers of our minds and bodies. After a while, we hear our elders say that certain of our traits are the reappearance of similar ones in grandpa or great-uncle Peter. So we know that our environment and heredity have limited our "freedom" greatly. Later, if we are believers, justified by Christ's blood, we learn to think of our lives, apart from God's saving grace, as a slavery to sin. Only the Son of God can make us free (see John 8:30-40).

Once we accept these truths, perhaps we are ready to understand that God has a greater hand in that power by which the world operates than we would think, apart from the scriptural revelation.

God's Complete Plan
God has a complete plan for the heavens and the earth which He created. Let us consider some of the scriptural evidences.

Perhaps the single greatest scriptural witness is in the widespread predictive prophecies of the Bible. The prophets told of coming events in Jewish history long before they came to pass. One, for example, was that the Jews would be made servants to the king of Babylon and after 70 years would be freed to return to their native land. Part of this is in Jeremiah's prophecy: " 'Behold, I will send and take all the families of the north,' saith the Lord, 'and Nebuchadnezzar the king of Babylon, My servant, and will bring them against this land . . . And this whole land shall be a desolation, and an astonishment; and these nations shall serve the king of Babylon seventy years. And it shall come to pass, when seventy years are accomplished, that I will punish the king of Babylon' " (Jer. 25:9, 11-12). About 70 years later (Jeremiah spoke just at the beginning of the 70 years) another prophet in Babylon read Jeremiah and waited expectantly to see what the older prophet had announced come to pass. And it did, as Daniel 9:1-3, Isaiah 44:21—45:3, 2 Chronicles 36:19-23 and Ezra 1 show.

Some might suppose that God merely noted what "natural laws or some such thing would bring to pass and by this "foreknowledge" told Isaiah, Jeremiah, and Daniel about it. But such is not the claim of God in Scripture. After a lengthy oracle on the future of two ancient kingdoms, Babylon and Assyria, Isaiah wrote: "The Lord of hosts hath sworn, saying, 'Surely as I have thought, so shall it come to pass; and as I have purposed, so shall it stand: that I will break the Assyrian in my land [see Isaiah 36—37 for the fulfillment] . . . This is the purpose that is purposed upon the whole earth: and this is the hand that is stretched out upon all the nations. For the LORD of hosts hath purposed, and who shall disannul it? and His hand is stretched out, and who shall turn it back?' " (Isa. 14:24-27)

Consider also Isaiah 46:9-10, "I am God, and there is none like Me, declaring the end from the beginning, and from ancient times the things that are not yet done, saying, 'My counsel shall stand, and I will do all My pleasure.' "

Men usually do not know they are carrying out God's plan. As they do their wicked deeds they think as the poet W. E. Henley did, in his well-known lines:

Invictus

Out of the night that covers me,
    Black as the pit from pole to pole,
I thank whatever gods may be
    For my unconquerable soul.

In the fell clutch of circumstance
    I have not winced, nor cried aloud.
Under the bludgeoning of chance
    My head is bloody, but unbowed.

Beyond this place of wrath and tears
    Looms but the horror of the shade;
And yet the menace of the years
    Finds, and shall find, me unafraid.

It matters not how strait the gate,
    How charged with punishments the scroll,
I am the master of my fate;
    I am the captain of my soul!

The wicked Assyrian king, furious against the kingdom of Israel, was completely unaware that he was an instrument of God's fury— "O Assyrian, the rod of mine anger . . . I will send him . . . against the people of My wrath . . . Howbeit he meaneth not so, neither doth his heart think so; but it is in his heart to destroy" (Isa. 10:5-7).

These passages are only a fraction of the biblical evidence that there is an "eternal plan by which God has rendered certain all the events of the universe, past, present, and future" (Strong, *Systematic Theology*, p. 353). "Known unto God are all His works from the beginning of the world" (Acts 15:18). Paul recognized a plan in history "predestinated according to the purpose of Him who worketh all things after the counsel of His own will" (Eph. 1:11).

God's plan goes by several biblical names and designations. Each of the terms emphasizes some aspect of the doctrine and is therefore helpful in understanding it. Notice the underlined words in the following Scripture quotations, each of them being a different, but apparent, designation of God's plan for His creation: "My *counsel* shall stand, and I will do all My *pleasure*" (Isa. 46:10): "*predestinated* according to His *purpose*" (Eph. 1:11; Rom. 8:28-29); "worketh all things according to the *counsel* of His *will* (Eph. 1:11; Dan. 4:35); "having *determined* their *appointed* times" (Acts 17:26, NASB); "*foreordained*" (1 Peter 1:20); "being *predestinated*" (Eph. 1:11; Rom. 8:30).

A Single, Comprehensive Plan

This plan of God is a single plan, for all parts of it exist together in God "with whom is no variableness, neither shadow of turning" (James 1:17). Scripture calls it "the purpose" of God (Eph. 1:11), not the "purposes."

The Christian thinker must be careful lest he fall into the error of *determinism*. Our own consciousness and the Bible both tell us we have some sort of freedom as human beings.

There are three basic kinds of determinism advocated in the world. This is to say, those who think men have no freedom propose one of these three causes for this lack. One is a sort of *impersonal, materialistic fate* thought to be built into the very fabric of the universe. This is the *moira, aisa*, or *fatum* (fate or fates) of Greek and Roman antiquity. The gods were "born" into a world already existing, a world directed by fate.

As the ancients became scientific, the second form of determinism—*cause-effect in an eternal chain*—arose and is still with us as *scientific determinism*, either environmental or hereditary or both. This was early joined, through astrology, with the first form. Both have had revivals in modern times and together reign on the university campus today.

A third form is *religious*, especially in Muslim, nontrinitarian, monotheism. Any strongly held monotheism which has no Saviour God, no wise, loving, holy Father, quickly becomes a harsh fatalism, as in the whole Muslim world. The same view develops in forms of Christianity where awareness of God's sovereignty is not matched with awareness of His love, mercy, and moral nature.

The plan of God, so often cited in Scripture, is always a spur to action, usually moral action as we shall see.

An Eternal Plan

This plan of God is, of course, eternal, never something improvised "in the nick of time"—never *ad hoc* or an expedient. God's actions sometimes surprise *us*, but He is never surprised. His plan, according to several passages, is an eternal plan (Eph. 3:11; James 1:17) which cannot be changed. True, "The Lord bringeth the counsel of the heathen to nought: he maketh the devices of the people of none effect," but not so His own plan, for "the counsel of the Lord standeth forever, the thoughts of His heart to all generations." And what a marvelous thing it is to be one of the Lord's people, knowing about His purpose: "Blessed is the nation whose God is the Lord; and the people whom He hath chosen for His own inheritance" (Ps. 33:10-12).

This single, eternal, all-inclusive plan becomes meaningful to believers as they consider the detail with which it is described in Scripture. Most of these details accompany some message of duty or comfort. God's plan is never presented in the Bible to relieve believers of hope or responsibility nor to discourage effort in the slightest way. We should not be surprised if some people say, "I don't see how you can believe this doctrine and still believe that you are morally responsible." Or, "How can God hold you responsible for either good or evil?" These questions arise when people misunderstand the doctrine.

Let's consider, therefore, the details of the plan which the Bible associates with God's *eternal purpose*.

1. God's plan includes the permanence and stability of the material universe, what scientists call the uniformity of nature. "Thy faithfulness is unto all generations; Thou hast established the earth, and it abideth. They continue this day according to Thine ordinances: for all [all things] are Thy servants" (Ps. 119:90-91). This is such a sure matter that the certainty of God's promises to His people is measured by the regularity and permanence of the

course of nature. Likewise, the essential unsearchableness of God's ways in nature is parallel with His unsearchable grace in redemption. All of this is in Jeremiah 31:35-37: "Thus saith the Lord, which giveth the sun for a light by day, and the ordinances of the moon and of the stars for a light by night, which divideth the sea when the waves thereof roar; the Lord of hosts is His name: 'If those ordinances depart from before Me,' saith the Lord, 'then the seed of Israel also shall cease from being a nation before Me forever.' Thus saith the Lord: 'if heaven above can be measured, and the foundations of the earth searched out beneath, I will also cast off the seed of Israel for all that they have done,' saith the Lord."

2. The plan of God specifically relates to the nations of the earth—their boundaries, governments, resources, history, and condition. We readily accept this of Israel, well known as an object of God's special attention. But God gives every nation its territory. The Horites and the Edomites (children of Esau) were given their land as God gave Israel theirs (Deut. 2:12). Furthermore, "When the Most High divided to the nations their inheritance, when He separated the sons of Adam [cf. Gen. 10:32], He set the bounds of the people" (Deut. 32:8). Paul is most direct on the point, saying to a Gentile audience, "God that made the world . . . hath made of one blood all nations of men for to dwell on all the face of the earth, and hath determined the times before appointed, and the bounds of their habitation" (Acts 17:24, 26). So, though both Kaiser Wilhelm and Adolph Hitler thought the German people needed more *Lebensraum* (room to live), God saw to it that, for a time at least, they were not to get it.

3. Also included in the plan is the precise length of each man's life. This is not a philosophy of "when your number is up"—far from it. Rather it is a truth designed to inculcate an attitude of peaceful confidence among God's children, delivering them from bondage to the fear of death (Heb. 2:15). Job was aware of this, commenting that man's "days are determined, the number of his months are with Thee [God], Thou hast appointed his bounds that he cannot pass" (Job 14:5). This teaches certain responsibilities contrary to what is popularly called fatalism. Moses said that

since God has numbered our days in His wisdom (Ps. 90:3-10) we should "number" them too. "So teach us," he prays, "to number our days, that we may apply our hearts unto wisdom" (Ps. 90:12).

I once heard a Free Methodist evangelist say, "Every man is immortal until his work is done," and he was undoubtedly right. This accounts in part for the cheerful, good hope of the Apostle Paul throughout the New Testament reports of his ministry, even when he was in prison for alleged capital crimes (Philippians). It accounts also for his quiet resignation to the end of his life, soon to come, knowing he had finished his divinely charted course and kept the faith (2 Tim. 4:6-8).

4. God's sovereign plan includes the circumstances under which we live—poverty or riches, labor or leisure, sickness or health, bad times or good, and the circumstances in which we die. So it is right for believers to learn to say, from the heart, "if the Lord will" about all plans for their future (see James 4:13-15). As great a man as the Apostle Paul found it right to submit his missionary plans to God, even when he might have had plans of his own (Rom. 1:10-13).

Modern people with their ideas about equality are frequently out of patience with any God who sanctions social and economic classes. Other generations have not felt this way. It is also hard for us to accept either ill health or poverty as the will of God for anybody. Let those who think this way read what Paul had to say about slaves (1 Cor. 7:20-24), unmarried people (vv. 25-26), the married who might wish to be free (v. 27), and the divorced (v. 27).

Sometimes preachers say that it is not God's will for anyone to be sick. If you think this, read Paul's words about sickness; it is sometimes God's will (2 Tim. 4:20; 2 Cor. 12:7-10). Poverty can be God's will for us too. Other generations have understood this better than ours. The Bible even has several examples of God's predetermination of how and when certain men, at least, would die (Abraham, Gen. 15:15; Jesus, John 2:19). Can we doubt that the same is true of us? One Psalm says, apparently of all, both beasts and men, "These wait all upon Thee . . . That Thou givest them, they gather . . . Thou hidest Thy face, they are troubled; Thou takest away their breath, they die, and return to their dust" (Ps. 104:27-29).

5. God's plan includes men's evil acts as well as their good ones. The Bible specifically says of the wicked deeds of Joseph's brothers in selling Joseph to traveling merchants (Gen. 37:23-28) that though they meant evil "God meant it unto good" (Gen. 50:20, cf. Ps. 105:17 and Gen. 45:4-8). Similar interpretations are given by the Bible to the hardening of Pharaoh's heart, and even the betrayal and shameful execution of Jesus. Judas had a part in God's plan! (See Jesus' comments, John 17:12; Mark 14:18-21.)

The jealous Jewish leaders, who were responsible for the Crucifixion, were part of God's plan too. Peter told them this plainly: "Ye men of Israel . . . Jesus of Nazareth, a man approved of God among you . . . Him, being delivered by the determinate counsel and foreknowledge of God, ye have taken, and by wicked hands have crucified and slain" (Acts 2:22-23). The fact that the wicked deeds of these parties to crime were all in God's plan, some even predicted in Scripture, in no wise relieved the men who did those things from guilt and punishment for them. This is plain in each case, especially Judas'—"Good were it for that man if he had never been born."

We must understand that, though the decrees are different, some causative and gracious, others permissive and just, both the judgment of the impenitent and the salvation of the believing are in the plan of God. "Unto you therefore which believe He is precious," wrote Peter, "but unto them which be disobedient, the stone which the builders disallowed, the same is made the head of the corner, and a stone of stumbling, and a rock of offense, even to them which stumble at the word, being disobedient: whereunto also they were appointed" (1 Peter 2:7-8).

Questions and Problems
Now, if we grant that the biblical teaching has been fairly presented, we may raise some questions which should, if possible, be answered. We cannot answer all the questions which the mind can raise. God's ways are not our ways nor His thoughts ours.

Our part is to believe that what God says to be true is true. Only after that do we attack the problems.

The most serious question relates to *freedom*. How can there be freedom of choice if God has decreed all that shall happen, from the fall of raindrops and sparrows to the rise of stars and empires? We find no insuperable difficulty if we observe a distinction between the decrees and their execution.

God made the decrees but He does not externally compel people to do either right or wrong. Responsible men carry out the decrees, voluntarily. If they are slaves to sin, as Jesus said, that is hardly God's fault. One thinks of the sons of Eli—"sons of Belial; they knew not the Lord" (1 Sam. 2:12). They were rebuked by their father for their gross sins. But, says the Scripture, most significantly, "Notwithstanding they harkened not unto the voice of their father, because the Lord would slay them" (1 Sam. 2:25). Thus the doctrine is confirmed; without any compulsion from God or men these young men freely chose to do the evil which destroyed them (see 4:17).

Men do not agree on what freedom is. I am indebted to *Our Daily Bread,* published by Radio Bible Class, for a very helpful tale in this regard.

"The story is told about the members of a congregation who got into a squabble one day over the issue of predestination and free will. While the controversy raged, the people separated, going to opposite sides of the auditorium. One man, not knowing which group to join, slipped into the predestination crowd. But he didn't stay long. Someone asked him, 'Who sent you here?' He replied, 'No one, I came of my own free will.' This brought the angry response, 'What? You can't be one of us and talk that way.' Quickly he was shoved across the aisle. But now he was questioned about his reasons for joining the free-will group. When he said, 'I was forced over here,' they indignantly shouted, 'Get out! You can't join us unless you choose to do so.' This poor believer was shut out from his brothers and sisters because they were fighting over a problem that's beyond the full grasp of man's puny little mind."

Some theologians try to modify predestination by referring certain fulfillment of the decrees of God to His foreseeing the events, thus making foresight the foundation of *predestination*.

That *foreknowledge,* in the sense of foresight, has a place in the decrees cannot be doubted. But if foresight is made dependent on God's knowledge of the laws of men and things, as some argue, we need to remember that God made the laws, and He, therefore, insures the results.

Does this understanding of predestination make God the author of sin? By no means. Sinners are the authors of sin. They are not coerced to sin. They do so voluntarily. God even preserves them in life while they follow self-chosen paths. God overrules their evil for good but He holds all evildoers guilty.

The divine decree of sin is not *efficient;* it is only *permissive.* Why God permitted Satan to tempt Eve, why He allowed evil at all is, of course, an indissoluble mystery. He could have prevented it, but He did not. To allow sin *now* is only an extension of the decree to allow sin in the first place.

With all its mystery, the biblical story provides the best answer to the meaning of life. Alternatives to the biblical doctrine are simply unacceptable. All, without exception, lead to errors. The chief errors are the denial of original sin (and the universally corrupt human nature, depravity) and the doctrine of a limited God.

This teaching, rightly expounded, however, has had great influence for good in Christian communities. It promotes a solemn but joyful confidence that with the future in God's hands, the story of our race will indeed "come out right" in the end. Romans 8:28 is truth, not just overheated enthusiasm. People who deeply believe this tend to be steady, productive citizens of the community. They know that "our labor is not in vain in the Lord." Awareness of God's plan inculcates humility in the face of *His complete sovereignty over the past, the present and the future.* It should cause the unbelieving and impenitent to be aware that their sins, too, are in God's calculations. They will never "get away with" a thing. He will bring every deed to judgment. The sinner, therefore, is pointed to the means of God's grace that he may learn of Him, believe, and be among those whom God counts His people—the redeemed of all the ages.

Many years ago Dorothea Day wrote a parody of "Invictus." Her piece is entitled "My Captain."

> Out of the light that dazzles me,
>   Bright as the sun from pole to pole,
> I thank the God I know to be
>   For Christ the conquerer of my soul.
>
> Since His the sway of circumstance
>   I would not wince nor cry aloud.
> Under the rule which men call chance
>   My head with joy is humbly bowed.
>
> Beyond this place of sin and tears—
>   That life with Him! and His the aid,
> That spite the menace of the years,
>   Keeps, and shall keep, me unafraid.
>
> I shall not fear though strait the gate;
>   He cleared from punishments the scroll.
> Christ is the Master of my fate;
>   Christ is the Captain of my soul.

10

God's Work of Creation

"Things which are seen were not made of things which do appear (Heb. 11:3).

There was a time when there was no world. It did not exist. The Psalm of Moses puts it this way, "Before the mountains were brought forth, or ever Thou hadst formed the earth and the world, even from everlasting to everlasting Thou art God" (Ps. 90:2). Several other passages speak of a time "before the world was" (John 17:5) and "before the foundation of the world" (John 17:24).

That the world had a beginning is assumed in all that the Scriptures say about such doctrines as decrees (predestination) and preservation. It is patent fact, and so obvious in the whole biblical world-and-life-view, that people who read and love the Bible can scarcely think in any other way about the world.

Simple observation teaches us that though the processes of regeneration and restoration are at work in nature, they do not quite restore nature. Most of the mountains are a little lower each year. The energy given off by the sun is never returned to it. The more sophisticated observations of science tell us the universe is spreading out and running down. This too, points to a beginning in finite time.

Wiseacres of our secularist age have nothing to say about the ultimate cause of nature. A few, contrary to the material evidences, speak vaguely of an eternally existing, uncaused world.

There have always been religious people who opposed the idea of a beginning of the world. This has usually taken one of two forms. One is the doctrine of God's *emanation*. In this view, the world is identical in substance with God, much as sunbeams are extensions of the reality of the source of all light, the sun. So things we see are little pieces of God, so to speak.

Folk who identify God with that they see in nature, rather than seeing nature as His work, are taking this view of things whether they know it or not. There are many anti-Christian implications. The doctrine of emanation virtually denies God's transcendence; and it compromises God's holiness by making all evil a part of Him.

Ancient gnosticism, a system which tried to interpret Christianity in the forms of Eastern theosophy, taught emanationism. It has always been a temptation to the mystically inclined, that is, to people who seek direct routes to God through meditation and ascetic practices apart from the historical Christ and God's Word.

Another form of denial of a divine beginning (and of Creation) is *dualism*. Dualism teaches that God (thought of as an idea) and matter, though distinct from one another, have always existed and always shall. Since both God (or Mind or Spirit) and matter are eternal, the world had no beginning. Dualism is an effort to explain the presence of evil by attaching it to material things, but it has too many conflicts with Christian principles to be acceptable.

Absolute Beginning

The universe was brought into existence by the one, true, eternal God out of no materials at all. There was an absolute beginning of things.

"In the beginning God created the heaven and the earth" (Gen. 1:1). These words take us back to the time when, in the presence of nothing outside the Godhead, God brought the heaven and the earth into existence. "Through faith we understand that the worlds were framed by the Word of God, so that things which are seen were not made of things which do appear" (Heb. 11:3).

Sometimes, this act or series of acts is defined as creating "out of nothing *(ex nihilo)*. This is acceptable as long as we remember that "nothing" must not be regarded as a "something." This error is found in classical Greek philosophy, frequently as formlessness, a source of evil, and in modern existentialism as the principle opposing authenticity.

Genesis 1:1 does not say that God used no materials in His creative work. But if it is an absolute beginning to which Moses refers, then the situation requires "out of nothing." The context and the nature of the idea must decide for us.

There are important reasons for accepting Genesis 1:1 as the absolute beginning of the universe. Later Scriptures seem to understand it in that way. (See Prov. 8:23; John 1:1, 2; Heb. 1:10.) The summary of creation events in Genesis 2:1-4a seems to presuppose that the story found in Genesis 1:1 to the end of the chapter begins with an act of God in creating the world absolutely. Efforts to change the translation to "In the beginning of God's creating the heavens and the earth, the earth was" are unsuccessful (J. O. Buswell, *Systematic Theology,* I, 147-150).

The Method of God in Creation

We live in an age that likes to think of itself as scientific. Science is interested in methods, so people want to know *how* God created the world. Did He do it all at once? Once He created matter and energy did the rest evolve by laws He created with the matter and energy? By the nature of the case we can't answer these questions for certain. First, creation out of nothing is a miracle. Once the "natural" causes for an event are explained it ceases to be a miracle. Second, try as the astronomers, geologists, and physicists may, they can never know how God created. There are several competing "scientific" models of creation. However one decides to interpret the six days of the Genesis creation narrative, it is clear that God ended the work of creating things when the epoch was over. According to Genesis 2:1-3, God rested (ceased) from His finished work of creation.

Preservation continues, but His methods are probably different in this present work than in His original creating. Hence, though the scientist may learn much about present-day natural processes, he can never be quite sure that they prevailed in Creation—whether it took a moment, six 24-hour days, or a hundred billion years. The processes he observes now relate to God's works of preservation and providence, not to His work of Creation. By revelation we know several things about the methods God used, but even what revelation tells us relates more to things modern men seldom ask about. Here are several of them:

1. *God employed His wisdom in creating.* In Proverbs 8, Wisdom, represented as a female, stands in a prominent place, and cries, "The Lord possessed me in the beginning of His way, before His works of old" (v. 22). Then, Wisdom claims to have been present at the various stages of Creation, assisting at each juncture (vv. 27-31). "He hath established the world by His wisdom . . . by His discretion" (Jer. 10:12b). "O Lord, how manifold are Thy works [creation and preservation]; in widom hast Thou made [created] them all" (Ps. 104:24). The functional efficiency of the Creation, including the starry heavens, testifies to God the Creator's intelligence.

2. *God employed His power in creating.* This seems so evident, even apart from texts which assert it, that it scarcely can be doubted. David was impressed with the creative power of God when he wrote, "The firmament [the expanse of space] showeth His handiwork" (Ps. 19:1).

As a young pastor, I built most of a church house with my own hands. The walls were of 12-inch concrete blocks, each weighing in excess of 60 pounds. The size of the building was 52 feet by 64 feet. How my muscles ached during those 14 months! To this day I never pass the large masonry construction without silently calculating the power necessary to put the stones in place. The first time I saw the gigantic, dressed Herodian stones at Hebron—several feet in each dimension—I had to ponder them quietly for several minutes to estimate their weight. What power it took to put them in place! But God put the lights in the expanse of heaven

—the greater to rule the day, the lesser to rule the night. He "made the stars also" (Gen. 1:14-18) and has been, by preservation, keeping them in place ever since. "He . . . hangeth the earth upon nothing" (Job 26:7). "He hath made the earth by His power" (Jer. 10:12).

3. *God employed His will in creating.* The 24 elders of John's vision say to God: "For Thou didst create all things, and because of Thy will they existed and were created" (Rev. 4:11, NASB). This probably means that the various aspects of creation are the execution of God's eternal decree. Will is the nearest thing we, God's only rational earth-creatures, have to creative power. We can create ideas in the mind without apparent reduction of energy. And these ideas are, in the case of some of the more artistic of our number, the finest work we do, for the ideas are parents of works like Rembrandt's paintings or Borglum's statuary or the Grand Coulee Dam.

4. *God employed His Word in creating.* Many times the formula, "And God said, 'Let there be' . . . and there was," appears in the familiar narrative. The Bible reader naturally connects this with Hebrews 11:3, "The worlds were framed by the Word of God" and with other texts such as "By the Word of the Lord were the heavens made; and all the host of them by the breath of His mouth . . . For He spake, and it was done; He commanded, and it stood fast" (Ps. 33:6, 9): "For He commanded, and they were created" (Ps. 148:5). The Word of God may be written (the Scriptures), spoken (as at Jesus' baptism), or Incarnated Word (as the Son of God in the first chapter of John). There may be other senses. But all of them derive from the familiar phenomenon of human language through which we communicate ideas, commands, and wishes.

Some serious-minded Christians think that when we find expressions like these, *immediate* application of divine power is always intended. Secondary or mediate causes are not in view. So the creation of the world had to be by a succession of instantaneous divine fiats—spoken commands—without any passage of time and without employment of means of any sort. Several recent books employing considerable show of scholarship attempt to prove that in the biblical texts which speak of creation by God's Word (mouth, breath, command), the Bible specifically means immediate (without means), instantaneous creation and nothing else.

It is worth noting, however, that this has not been the view of some first-rate conservative scholars. Many of them think the opposite, that God used means and extended time in His creating work. If this view is not specifically taught in the Bible it is at least allowed.

The belief that the six days of Creation in the first chapter of Genesis must be interpreted as six literal 24-hour days as we know days and nights, evenings and mornings, has not been characteristic of the great teachers and the church of the past. It seems rather to be the child of modern controversy.

One modern, respected, and devout writer says: "Respecting the length of the six creative days, speaking generally, . . . the patristic [Church Fathers] and medieval exegesis makes them to be long periods of time, not days of twenty-four hours. The latter interpretation has prevailed *only in the modern church.* Augustine teaches that the length of the six days is not to be determined by the length of our weekdays. Our seven days, he says, resemble the seven days of the account in Genesis, in being a series, and in having the vicissitudes of morning and evening . . . He calls attention to the fact that the 'six or seven days may be, and are called six days, God-divided days,' in distinction from 'sun-divided days.' Anselm remarks that there was a difference of opinion in his time" (Shedd, *Dogmatic Theology,* I, pp. 475-476, italics added). Shedd adds that there is merit in the suggestion that "the seven days of the human week are copies of the divine week. Thus 'sun-divided days' are images of 'God-divided days' " (p. 477).

Surely God's word of creation does not *necessarily* mean immediate, instantaneous creation. One of the most important texts is 2 Timothy 3:16 which says all Scripture is *theopneustos,* literally "God-breathed." Conservative scholars everywhere accept the evidence adduced and summarized by B. B. Warfield, the Princeton scholar at the turn of the twentieth century, that the breath of God and similar expressions (command, mouth) refer simply to His creative acts.

In the case of Holy Scripture, we know God used both time and human means in producing His written revelation. At least several dozen human authors wrote during 1500 years in producing the 66 books. So God's breath, command, word, and mouth, must indicate *God's creative power in action, by whatever means and taking whatever time needed.* The Bible really says little specifically about the means God employed. On the other hand, neither does the so-called geological or astronomical record. Theories about the means and time employed will always remain just that—theories. We do not have sufficient revelation regarding the means of Creation and the time of it to construct a dogma about the week. It was a God-divided week; whether a sun-divided week or not is not ours to say until God says so.

The Purpose of Creation

Why did God create the world? Today's secular writers do not concern themselves with purposes. If, as they suppose, there is no reality outside the material world, locked up in its cause-effect sequences, then there is no goal for nature or history. An important text of Scripture speaks to the contrary: "The Lord has made everything for its own purpose" (Prov. 16:4, NASB). The purpose in view in this verse may be an immediate one; for example, the sun to shine, eyes to see, ears to hear, fins for swimming, and legs for walking. But each immediate purpose was intended to serve one ultimate purpose for the whole of creation. That purpose may be summed up in three short statements, each scripturally derived.

1. The *chief end* of creation is God, Himself, "For of Him, and through Him, and to Him are all things: to whom be glory for ever. Amen" (Rom. 11:36). God's design is, as Paul puts it, "that God may be all in all" (1 Cor. 15:28, Isa. 48:11). From what we know of creativity in ourselves, we would suppose that

the Maker's own satisfaction is a primary goal in creativity, but not that it is the only one.

2. The goal of God for Himself, in creation, is the manifestation of His perfections. The Bible calls this His will, or His pleasure. James Orr pointed out that the creation of man had a distinct place in God's scheme for displaying His own perfections: "Till a mind of this kind appeared, capable of surveying the scene of its existence, of understanding the wisdom and beauty displayed in its [creation's] formations, and of utilizing for rational purposes the vast resources laid up in its treasuries, the very existence of such a world as this remained an inexplicable riddle: an adequate final cause . . . was not to be found in it" (*The Christian View of God and the World,* Eerdmans, 1948, p. 135). Orr goes on to say, "There is a delight which creative wisdom has in its own productions, which is an end in itself. God saw the works that He had made, and behold they were good; though not until man appeared on the scene were they declared 'very good.' "

3. This idea leads to another—God created the world for His own glory. All of God's works are for this purpose. In the achievements of this goal all other goals are attained. That His own glory was God's goal in Creation is the plain truth of Scripture and is demonstrable by reason as well.

In the first place, when God purposed to create He did so before any creature existed. The reason, therefore, must lie in God Himself, not in the nonexisting creature. The absolute cannot be subordinate to the finite.

Secondly, God is a more worthy being than the sum of all creation. His own excellence on display is worthier than the excellence or happiness of all of creation.

Thirdly, even among ourselves as men, the excellency of our makings and doings—be it building a better mousetrap or running a faster mile—is rightly attributed to the maker and doer. The same is surely true of God, the master Maker and Doer, and His creation.

Finally, the securing of the Creator's glory as the *chief end* not only of man but of all creatures, secures also their own highest good, happiness, and excellence. A. H. Strong has written: "His own glory is an end which comprehends and secures, as a subordinate end, every interest of the universe. The interests of the universe are bound up in the interests of God. There is no holiness or happiness for creatures except as God is absolute sovereign, and is recognized as such. It is therefore not selfishness, but benevolence, for God to make His own glory the supreme object of creation. Glory is not vain-glory, and in expressing this ideal, that is, in expressing Himself, in His creation, He communicates to His creatures the utmost possible good" (*Systematic Theology,* p. 400).

It is the duty of men, then, to adopt God's goal as their own: "Whether therefore ye eat, or drink, or whatsoever ye do, do all to the glory of God" (1 Cor. 10:31; see 1 Peter 4:11).

A Question about Creation

One question often occurs to people who become acquainted with the biblical view of Creation. How can we explain evil in a world that the holy God has made?

The presence of sin is never explained in the Bible. We know how the human race fell into it. It came through a wrong exercise of God-given freedom by our common father, Adam. "As by one man sin entered into the world . . . For as by one man's disobedience many were made sinners" (Rom. 5:12, 19). Since sin is in the race through Adam's sin, it is, in this sense, here by God's permission.

But Genesis says nothing about the ultimate source of sin. The presence of the serpent or Satan is never explained in the Bible. Since God is the Creator of all, Satan must be a creature of God's making and since all was once good, Satan, like man, must have changed. But evil remains an unsolved riddle. We only know that God alone is omnipotent and He has future plans for His world.

The doctrine of Creation holds a number of mysteries. We need to beware of those who insist that we must agree with their theories in every detail or else be sub-Christian and less than loyal to biblical revelation. We will be wise to commit ourselves irrevocably to none of the theories. Creation is a miracle. As such, it is a divine mystery. We can never penetrate it, though we may trust all that God has said about it.

11

The Creation of Unseen Spirits

"All things . . . visible and invisible . . . created by Him" (Col. 1:16).

Though we live in a world of sights and sounds, there is about us another world, of unseen spirits. Several exalted passages in the New Testament place this world of created spirits squarely before us. One of these urges: "Put on the whole armour of God, that ye may be able to stand against the wiles of the devil. For we wrestle not against flesh and blood, but against principalities, against powers, against the rulers of the darkness of this world, against spiritual wickedness in high places" (Eph. 6:11-12).

Evidently, to help his readers shun the worship of these spirits, Paul spoke of Christ's victory at the Cross as a triumph over certain "principalities and powers" (Col. 2:15). In Ephesians, the Apostle described these spirits as "wicked." They rule "the dark world" and are in "high places." Paul calls them princes (principalities) with great power. Although they have been "defeated" by Christ, they are nevertheless to be "conquered" by us too, when we employ the whole panoply of spiritual armor—truth, righteousness, the Gospel of peace, faith, salvation, the Spirit, the Word and prayer (Eph. 6:13-18).

These Pauline summaries seem to relate to evil spirits. His letters furnish no similar discussions of unseen good spirits, who help rather than oppose the Christian. Elsewhere in the Bible, however, from Genesis to Revelation, they frequently appear, though almost always as incidental to the biblical story. These spirits frequently appear as men, apparently dressed according to the styles of the times. But aside from this, later visual representations of them in art seem to be without biblical foundation. Scripture uses pronouns in the masculine gender to refer to them but it specifically says that they are without sexual features or functions. The wings almost always appearing in pictures of angels are without scriptural foundation, except for a certain class of spiritual beings called seraphs (Isa. 6:2). These may or may not be angels. So it is wise to start with the Bible and leave our speculation about angels until we understand the scriptural evidence.

These unseen spirits, whether good or bad, go under a number of names in Scripture: angels, archangels, demons, devil, sons of God, seraphs, watchers. Three of them have personal names: Gabriel, Michael, and Satan. There is no clear information whether the single generic name most common, angel (Heb. *mal-'ak,* Gr. *angelos*), meaning messenger, applies to all of them or not. Several of the most respected modern authorities treat all of the spirits as angels (Strong, A. Hodge, C. Hodge, Pieper, Mueller).

Origin of Angels

The origin of these spiritual creatures is clear in Scriptures. By Christ, we read, "were all things created, that are in heaven and that are in earth, visible and invisible, whether they be thrones, or dominions, or principalities, or powers: all things were created by Him and for Him" (Col. 1:16; 1 Peter 3:22). Outside of the Christian world, it is news to people that there is only one eternal, immortal Spirit (1 Tim. 3:16) and that all others have been created by Him and are under His control. This truth is the reason that angels, demons, and Satan usually appear in theological books under the rubric, "The Works of God: Creation."

Nature of Angels

It is also clear from Scripture that these beings (specifically angels) are persons—intelligent voluntary agents. They function as persons. The angel who appeared to Peter (Acts 12:7-10) functioned in every way as a human being would, tapping him awake, raising him up, speaking instructions, and leading him out of a building into a street. They are said to have wisdom (2 Sam. 14:20) and they have moral character, either holy (Mark 8:38) or sinful (2 Peter 2:4).

Whether angels have bodies or not is debated. They are called "spirits," a word used sometimes to designate the souls of men after death (1 Peter 3:19). We also know that angels have no sexual parts or functions. Jesus Himself said so (Luke 20:34-36; Mark 12:25). Thus, they are not a race propagated from a single original pair as the human race is. They must have been created individually. The Bible also says that they are deathless (Luke 20:36) and are not "flesh and blood" (Eph. 6:12). When they appeared in the Scripture narrative they sometimes looked like men and sometimes ate food, lodged, and spoke as men do. People even mistook them for men (Gen. 18:8, 19:3). On occasion an angel appeared as a man with a frightening, glorious appearance (Dan. 10:5-6; Judges 13:3, 6, 10-11) and acted in some amazing way (Judges 13:19). Sometimes they "flew swiftly" (Dan. 9:21)— by what means we do not know—and sometimes they were tardy (Dan. 10:13).

It seems clear that angels belong to a realm (call it spiritual, supernatural, eschatological) where body and form exist (witness Christ's glorified body) but not in the same mode as flesh-and-blood people. Jesus' risen body could masticate food (Luke 24:41-42); He had "flesh and bones" (Luke 24:39). Yet in that body He ascended to heaven and will come again. Some theologians suggest that angels have bodies similar to the risen body of Jesus; others believe that they are pure spirits who assume bodies for specific reasons. In light of this, the question should be left open.

Order of Angelic Beings

Angels are, however, a class of intelligent, spirit beings different from either God or men. They are "all ministering spirits" (Heb.

1:14; Ps. 104:4). Men are spiritual beings too, but angel spirits are inferior to men in order of being in some respects, since they are for the service of men, as Hebrews 1:14 indicates.

On the other hand, they are in some other respect superior to men. Peter compares them with human beings—certain false teachers—and says, "Angels, which are greater in power and might, bring not railing accusation against them" (2 Peter 2:11; see v. 1). Evidently, in knowledge and power, they are superior to us. Jesus spoke of them as having great knowledge—"of that day and hour knoweth no man, not the angels of heaven" (Matt. 24:36) and Peter wrote of their "power and might" (2 Peter 2:11).

They are, however, of limited knowledge and power. They are not divine beings. In another place Peter described them as seekers after information (1 Peter 1:12). Two passages tell us that they do not know as much as God knows (Matt. 24:36; Mark 13:32).

These facts—that angels are more powerful and of greater knowledge than men yet strictly limited in knowledge and power, incomparably inferior to God—explain why some people have been tempted to worship them (Col. 2:18) and why it is wrong to do so. This is enforced by still another revealed fact: men shall be their judges at some future time. Paul wrote, in a passage designed to convince believers of their competence to "judge" matters of congregational controversy, "Know ye not that we shall judge angels? How much more things that pertain to this life?" (1 Cor. 6:3)

While on the subject of their relation to God and men, it is appropriate to raise the question of ranks among themselves. Are there ranks and orders of angels? In the democratic atmosphere of our country, where manners, dress and language tell us very little about social position, this question may not occur without some prompting. Yet American democracy is almost without precedent and is a relatively recent development.

The Bible speaks of an archangel (1 Thes. 4:16; Jude 9), of thrones, dominions, principalities, and powers (Eph. 1:21; Col. 2:15), and indicates that one angel is a chief prince (Dan. 10:13).

Some of them are specially related to the devil and some to Michael (Rev. 12:7-9). Gabriel, probably an archangel (Dan. 9:21; Luke 1:26; 1 Thes. 4:16), is described as standing in the presence of God (Luke 1:19). So, though we do not know exactly what their lines of authority and positions of honor are, we know there are such positions. We also know that they respect rank (see Jude 9).

Activities of Angels

We may be sure that in any God-ordered society (see 1 Cor. 11:2, 34; 14:33, 40) position and rank will serve useful purposes—work is one of them. What do good angels do? A search of the Scriptures on this matter turns up an amazing mass of information. Angels are mentioned in about 275 passages of Scripture, in at least 17 Old Testament books and 17 in the New. We discover that at least six tasks or services appear to occupy angels on a regular basis— perhaps constantly. The first three ministries are addressed to God: They praise God, they worship Him and they rejoice in His work.

John writes of seven spirits before God's throne (Rev. 1:4). Though these may symbolize the third person of the Godhead, we do know that certain angels do stand in God's presence (Luke 1:19). If the seraphs of Isaiah 6:2 are considered angels, worship is clearly involved. Other passages are specific (Ps. 148:1-2; Ps. 29:1-2; Job 38:6-7). Job indicates that angels (sons of God) were created long before man was and therefore were present to praise God and rejoice in God's creative activity.

Psalm 103:19-22 says God has a universal kingdom and broadly hints that in this kingdom His messengers (Hebrew word is the standard one rendered angels) do His bidding as "ministers of state," so to speak, executing God's commandments throughout "all places of His dominion." All governments require services of this kind. Paul once suggested that angels are spectators of earthly affairs and the name "watcher" (Dan. 4:13, 17, 23) clearly implies this.

Angels are prominently mentioned in connection with the coming and career of Christ. An angel predicted His birth (Matt. 1:20; Luke 1:26-38) as well as the birth of His forerunner, John (Luke 1:11-20) and later, angels announced Jesus' birth (Luke 2:8-14). Not long afterward, an angel warned Jesus' parents of the evil intent of King Herod (Matt. 2:13).

Angels attended Christ to aid Him at the beginning of His ministry (Matt. 4:11) and again near the end of it to strengthen Him (Luke 22:43). It may be significant that though Jesus could have called upon "legions of angels" to help Him at any time (Matt. 26:53), the Gospels never mention angelic aid except at the end of the temptations by the devil and during the agony of Gethsemane. We know they also had services to perform at the time of the Resurrection (Matt. 28:2, 6) and possibly at Jesus' ascension to heaven, for the "cloud" which "received Him out of their sight" may have been a "crowd" of angels, so at least some scholars suggest. Angels are presently devoted to the praise and worship of our Lord (Rev. 5:11-12). And He will come again "with clouds," we read, attended by angels "in like manner" as the Apostles saw Him go (Matt. 25:31; 1 Thes. 4:16-17; Acts 1:9-11, Jude 14, NASB).

The Lord's second advent will be accompanied by considerable angel activity. The establishment of His kingdom will be effected, in part, by angelic work. Specifically, they shall, in a policelike action, gather unclean things and unclean, unqualified persons out of the world. In interpreting His parable of the tares, Jesus said, "The Son of Man shall send forth His angels, and they shall gather out of His kingdom all things that offend, and them which do iniquity; and shall cast them into a furnace of fire: there shall be wailing and gnashing of teeth" (Matt. 13:41-42).

Angels have some kind of special place in God's providential rule of the nations. God, we know, has decreed the bounds of their habitation, the rise and fall of their rulers and the course of their histories (Ps. 24:1; Isa. 40:15; Rom. 13:1). And He uses angels in the execution of His will for them.

The Book of Daniel is especially interesting in this regard. In a frightening dream, Kind Nebuchadnezzar (according to his own report) learned that God's watchers, or holy ones, decreed his own rise and fall and restoration (Dan. 4:17). In Daniel's vision, received during the third year of Cyrus the Great of Persia (Dan. 10:1), Daniel learned that there was an angelic prince designated for the kingdom of Persia (10:13), another for Greece (10:20) and still another for Israel (10:21; see 11:1). Some of these angels seem to be satanically assigned.

The first Book of the Bible, and the last, represent angels as God's messengers and instruments of both providential judgments now and in the final judgment to come. Angels announced the destruction of Sodom both to Abraham (Gen. 18) and to Lot (Gen. 19). They shall pour out the vials of God's wrath on mankind in the coming "wrath of God upon the earth" (Rev. 16:1-12). They shall bind the devil and incarcerate him at the beginning of the Millennium (Rev. 20:1-3).

Ministry of Angels to God's People

Angels also have a special ministry in God's care of believers. We have already noted how an angel rescued Peter from prison. "Are they not all ministering spirits, sent forth to minister for them who shall be heirs of salvation?" (Heb. 1:14) Whether each Christian has an angel assigned to him or each child or each church, as has been inferred from certain texts (Matt. 18:3, 10; Heb. 1:14; Rev. 1:20), is doubtful. But we do know that all God's angels are working for us. They are interested in our efforts in evangelism and aid in securing physical safety (Acts 5:19; 12:7-10) and are present to help at the time of death. Michael would not let the devil disturb the grave of Moses, whom God Himself had buried (Deut. 34:6; Jude 9) and the soul of the beggar Lazarus was carried by angels to Abraham's bosom (Luke 16:22).

These observations by no means exhaust the teachings of Scripture about the ministry of angels. We have raised, however, an important question: Is it possible that in our modernity we have neglected something here which we ought to recapture? God has said, "The angel of the Lord encampeth round about them that fear Him, and delivereth them" (Ps. 34:7).

In 1943, an evangelist-pastor named Bernard N. Schneider held a series of meetings in the church I served as pastor. While there, he told a story which he recently included in his book, *The World of Unseen Spirits* (Winona Lake, Ind.; BMH Books, 1975, p. 40).

> During the years of World War II we lived in Washington, D.C., . . . on a Monday afternoon in the spring of 1941 we took a drive toward the city of Baltimore . . . my wife and five-year-old daughter went along for the ride. There were no freeways and interstate roads in those days, and we drove out Bladensburg Road and old U. S. Highway 1, which was then the main road between Washington and Baltimore. When we arrived in the suburbs of Baltimore, we agreed we had gone far enough and decided to turn around. So I turned into a side street to my right at an intersection with a traffic light, turned around the next block and came back to the intersection. The traffic light turned green for us just before we got to it, and I proceeded to make the left turn to get back on the highway toward home. Just at that moment a peculiar sensation gripped me which urged me to stop. I did not hear a voice audibly, but there was an inner voice which I can best describe as a compelling urge which said: Stop. I did stop right in front of the green light which said: Go. And just then a large truck came through the red light from our left at a very high rate of speed. Had I not stopped at the green light, we would likely have been three dead people . . . What made me stop? I do not remember of ever doing that deliberately, except on that day. I believe it was an angel from the Lord looking after us.

Satan and Evil Angels

The Bible never makes a point of it, but the record is clear that the issues of freedom and moral responsibility were worked out in this universe long before the present order of the cosmos began. Someone (or many), long before Adam and Eve, tested the Law of God regarding obedience and confirmed holiness on the one hand, with disobedience and depravity on the other. When the Bible begins the narrative of the moral life, moral evil is already present.

The serpent, later clearly identified as Satan (Rev. 12:9) was there (Gen. 3:1-15). His evil moral influence won the first encounter. He appears in five books of the Old Testament (Genesis, 1 Chronicles, Job, the Psalms, and Zechariah, perhaps also Isaiah and Ezekiel) and 19 Books of the New. Twenty-five of the references to him in the Gospels are from the mouth of Jesus Himself.

The Bible also refers to other evil angels. Sometimes they are associated with Satan as their leader. Once they are called "the angels that sinned" (2 Peter 2:4).

These evil angels, in general, are not a major biblical theme, but the one called Satan, Devil, Serpent, Dragon, Tempter, Beelzebub, the god of this world, and several other designations, is a major theme. The names employed divulge his malevolent character.

The literature on the subject is vast. Among contemporary evangelical authors, the subject is treated with considerable verve by those who regard Isaiah 14 (a prophecy about the king of Babylon) and Ezekiel 28 (a prophecy about an ancient king of Tyre) as, in some important sense, about Satan, his primeval fall, his present state and activity, and his future judgment. The standard theology books are more reserved and tend to have little to say about Satan's origin. One of the better summaries is from an old standard work:

> Satan, like other finite beings can only be in one place at a time; yet all that is done by his agents being attributed to him, he appears to be practically ubiquitous.
>
> It is certain that at times at least they [Satan's agents] have exercised an inexplicable influence over the bodies of men, yet that influence is entirely subject to God's control (Job 2:7; Luke 13:16; Acts 10:38). They have caused and aggravated diseases, and excited appetites and passions (1 Cor. 5:5). Satan, in some sense, has the power of death (Heb. 2:14).

With respect to the souls of men, Satan and his angels are utterly destitute of any power either to change the heart or to coerce the will, their influence being simply moral, and exercised in the way of deception, suggestion, and persuasion. The descriptive phrases applied by the Scriptures to their working are such as "the deceivableness of unrighteousness," "power, signs, lying wonders," (2 Thes. 2:9-10); he transforms himself into "an angel of light" (2 Cor. 11:14). If he can deceive or persuade he uses "wiles" (Eph. 6:11); "snares" (1 Tim. 3:7); "depths, (Rev. 2:24); he "blinds the mind," (2 Cor. 4:4); "leads captive the will," (2 Tim. 2:26); and so "deceives the whole world" (Rev. 12:9). If he cannot persuade he uses "fiery darts," (Eph. 6:16) and "buffetings" (2 Cor. 12:7) (A. A. Hodge, *Outlines of Theology,* Eerdmans, 1949, pp. 255-256).

Demons

Unclean spirits, called demons, are particularly prominent in the Gospels. We should probably consider them wicked angels. No one is ever said to be possessed by an evil angel, but considering the "messenger" nature of all angels, it seems appropriate to identify demons with fallen angels, though specific proof is lacking.

The New Testament distinctly regards what is called "demon possession" as a reality. It is not the same as mental disease. Jesus addressed the demons as distinct from the possessed person and the persons as distinct from the demons. The various other ailments which Jesus healed, however, are not said to be caused by evil spirits—no "evil spirit" theory of disease can be found in the Gospels.

Furthermore, demon possession is not the same as demon influence. Through the susceptibility of us all to mental suggestions, they certainly have an open field for action, as Peter's foolish acceptance of a satanic suggestion shows (Mark 8:33). Ananias, who allowed Satan to fill his heart with a bad motive, is another example of demon influence on the mind (Acts 5:2). But demon possession is something else. The person "possessed" by the evil spirit is apparently powerless against the demon until liberated by the Lord of heaven and earth.

12

Preservation and Providence of God

"My Father worketh hitherto, and I work" (John 5:17).

The Christian ideal of joy is found in the Book of Philippians, "Rejoice in the Lord alway: and again I say, Rejoice" (4:4); "The Lord is at hand. Be careful for nothing" (4:5-6).

Jesus' own prevailing good humor set the pace for trusting contentment. In His famous description of faith (Matt. 6:25-34), He concluded, "Therefore do not be anxious for tomorrow; for tomorrow will care for itself. Each day has enough trouble of its own (6:34, NASB).

The foundation of this cheerful optimism is the biblical world-and-life view. Specifically, we understand *first,* that God made the world (Creation) "good . . . very good" (Gen. 1:10, 31); "He hath made everything beautiful in his time" (Ecc. 3:11); *secondly,* that this was according to a plan He formed in eternity (Decrees or Predestination) so that no emergencies would ever arise requiring patchwork maintenance; *thirdly,* that when He finished creating the world He immediately set about maintaining it (Preservation) in good order; and *fourthly,* that He is governing it in such a way as to accomplish His good goals (Providence). This is the biblical teaching and no one will ever improve on it as a prescription for joy, in spite of pain, illness, decrepitude and, ultimately, death.

131

The Doctrine of Preservation

Preservation (maintenance) is indeed a separate work from providence (government). Creation and preservation are distinguished in the following passage: "Thou, even Thou art Lord alone; Thou hast made heaven, the heaven of heavens, with all their host, the earth, and all things that are therein, the seas, and all that is therein, and Thou preservest them all" (Neh. 9:6).

Preservation is distinguished from providence in a less direct way, but just as definitely. Psalm 104, for example, is the psalm of preservation. It presents the whole cosmic order as operating by a continuous outflow of the divine energy. Psalm 103, on the other hand, is the psalm of providence, God's "kingdom ruleth over all" (v. 19).

We see these distinctions also in the ministry of Jesus. When, on a Sabbath, He challenged His enemies at the pool of Bethesda by healing a man, He reminded them that even though God rested on the seventh day from His creative work (Creation), both He and the Father were still working, but at other things. These are preservation and providence (John 5:16-17; Gen. 2:2).

The Work of the Son of God

Biblical information on God's work of preservation is impressive. We might consider first two direct statements relating this work to the Son of God: "And He is before all things, and in Him all things hold together" (Col. 1:17, NASB); "And He is the radiance of His glory and the exact representation of His nature, and upholds all things by the word of His power" (Heb. 1:3, NASB). Another passage says; "in Him [God] we live, and move, and have our being" (Acts 17:28). We learn, from Psalm 104, that this upholding maintenance and renewal extends to all nature—the heavens, weather, soil, plants, animals, and man.

The Integrity of Creation

The doctrine of preservation teaches us that God maintains the integrity of things, both simple (the periodic table of elements, the key of "C") and complex (H_2O, the solar system, laws of musical harmony). One author speaks of the "existence of the whole created universe" and its "laws, properties, powers, and processes." Another affirms that preservation is that continued exercise of divine energy by which the Creator upholds all His creatures in being, and in the possession of all those inherent qualities that He gave them at their creation.

The scriptural detail of this doctrine is truly amazing. We could start with the sky above: "Lift up your eyes on high, and behold who hath created [past tense] these things, that bringeth out . . . [present tense] all by names by the greatness of His might, for that He is strong in power; not one faileth" (Isa. 40:26). Job and his friends add that "In whose [God's] hand is the soul of every living thing" (Job 12:9).

Psalm 104 starts with a pictorial representation of God presiding over the weather (vv. 1-4). It continues with God's gracious care for all His earthly creatures. He provides water for the beasts (vv. 10-13), and grasses for the cattle and trees for birds. He causes mountains and crags to rise up for wild goats and badgers (vv. 14-18). The heavenly bodies mark the seasons; night is for wild beasts to stalk their prey; day for their sleep and for man's work (vv. 19-23). Birth and death are within God's power as well as the sequence of the seasons.

The lines from Gray's *Elegy* are not strictly true.

Full many a flower of purest ray serene
    The dark unfathomed caves of ocean bear
Full many a flower is born to blush unseen
    And waste its sweetness on the desert air.

God has a place for all good things and employs them to support His plan.

A Continuous Work

God's work of preservation is never represented in Scripture as simply as the ticking of a cosmic clock, wound up at Creation but now unwinding. Some people think that it is unreasonable to suppose that God would be personally concerned with the innumerable details of millions of human lives, to say nothing of all existing things. That conviction, however, that God is sustaining us, His people, imparts the *religious* value to the Christian idea of God. "I can do all things through Christ which strengtheneth me" (Phil. 4:13); "The eternal God is thy refuge, and underneath are the everlasting arms" (Deut. 33:27).

Jesus taught His disciples to live in the light of this truth. "Do not be anxious for your life, as to what you shall eat, or what you shall drink; nor for your body, as to what you shall put on. . . . Look at the birds of the air, that do not they sow neither do they reap, nor gather into barns, and yet your heavenly Father feeds them. Are you not worth much more than they?" (Matt. 6:25-26, NASB) "Are not two sparrows sold for a cent? And yet not one of them will fall to the ground apart from your Father . . . Therefore do not fear, you are of more value than many sparrows" (Matt. 10:29, 31, NASB). Comforting, quotable, reliable, psychic medicine such as these passages is not available in any religion in which God is Creator only. He must act concurrently with us as well.

We know too that God sustains evil men in their ways—not because they are evil, but because they are His creatures. "God concurs with the evil acts of His creatures only as they are natural acts, not as they are evil" (A. H. Strong, *Systematic Theology*, p. 418).

A Gracious Work

This gracious work of God in preservation may be regarded as an aspect of His faithfulness, love, and mercy for all, but especially for the human race. The sun, moon, and stars go through their motions at the right times. Spring ever returns after winter. "While the earth remaineth" (Gen. 8:22) lovers marry, families are born, science and industry operate; indeed, life goes on, because God is faithful to maintain His creation. David summed it up: "Thy mercy, O Lord, is in the heavens; and Thy faithfulness reacheth unto the clouds. Thy rightousness is like the great mountains; Thy judgments are a great deep: O Lord, Thou preservest man and beast. How excellent is Thy lovingkindness, O God! Therefore the children of men put their trust under the shadow of Thy wings" (Ps. 36:5-7).

The Doctrine of Providence

Providence is the continuous exercise of God's power through which He causes all things in the created universe to fulfill the purpose for which God created them.

Creation explains how there happened to be a world at all; *Preservation* explains why it still exists in good order and *Providence* explains how it will develop toward God's eternally planned goal. It is the completion in time of the plan of God made in eternity.

The Bible seems to suggest that providence originates with God's *foreknowledge*. This is more than mere information in the sense that God knows what He prefers to do. Foreknowledge is God's act of informing His will. Although there is no temporal "process" in God's mind, we may think of a logical order in His plan and action. In this sense, we can speak of a "process" which involves God's *planning* (decrees) to do what He knows His will is; then through *creation,* next *preservation* and finally *providence,* events come to pass.

An Example of Providence

We can take a biblical, historical incident as an example of providence (2 Sam. 15—18). We know from many texts that God planned to rule Israel through David for a time and, more importantly, to bring Christ into the world through David. At one point, however, a rebellious son, Absalom, planned to destroy David. Ahithophel and Hushai were the king's counselors. When David was forced to flee Jerusalem both advisors stayed behind— Ahithophel willingly, for he joined Absalom's rebellion; Hushai at David's request. Not long afterward Ahithophel gave Absalom *good* advice, if Absalom was to destroy his father; Hushai gave *bad* advice, knowing it was bad and hoping thereby to destroy Absalom and to save David. Absalom followed the bad advice of Hushai, lost the battle, lost his kingdom, and lost his life, while

Ahithophel went to his home city, put his business affairs in order, and hanged himself.

Now God was not far away in heaven simply letting history unwind according to certain immutable laws of men and things. No man's freedom was limited by God. Every man—Joab, Ahithophel, Hushai, the elders, and the men of Absalom's party— did what he voluntarily decided to do. Yet, says the Scripture, "And Absalom and all the men of Israel said, 'The counsel of Hushai the Archite is better than the counsel of Ahithophel.' For the Lord had appointed to defeat the good counsel of Ahithophel, to the intent that the Lord might bring evil [a disastrous defeat] upon Absalom" (2 Sam. 17:14).

Regular Methods and Means of Providence
The Bible indicates at least three ways through which God regularly executes His work of providential control. First and most obvious is through supernatural miracles and "special" uses of natural forces. God saved Jerusalem during Hezekiah's reign through a supernatural plague (Isa. 37:36-38); He redeemed the Israelites from Egypt through a succession of 11 wonders—10 plagues and the parting of the Red Sea; He led them into Canaan by stopping the waters of the Jordan, breaking down the walls of Jericho, and causing the sun to stand still for several hours. Granted, some of these wonders were accomplished by use of natural forces—an east wind helped at the Red Sea (Ex. 14:21). Yet each was God's act in an extraordinary way.

In these cases, man's free will is maintained even as God controls the circumstances. Pharaoh and his army, for example, chose to follow the Israelites, yet as soon as they got into the trap of the sea bed, God released the waters to destroy them.

The miracles of the virgin birth of Jesus and His resurrection, like His death in our place, were planned in eternity and executed in time. If, however, Augustus had not decreed his census (Luke 2:1-5) and if Herod had not sought the young Child's life, Jesus would never have fulfilled the prophecies involving both Bethlehem and Egypt (Matt. 2:19-23). Neither Augustus nor Herod was coerced in any way to do what he did. Somehow, providence embraces both the free will of men and the eternal plan of God.

A second means of providence is the regular process of nature. Psalm 148:8 speaks of fire and hail, snow, vapors, and stormy winds fulfilling God's Word. People are not offended by this—unless they think deeply. It is easy to say that God sent the snow flurry to Waterloo in Belgium, over a century and a half ago, to defeat Napoleon. Or to say God kept the English Channel calm for several days to allow the defeated British army to escape Hitler's hosts in the early days of World War II. But few approve the suggestion that the Chicago fire may have been caused by God, especially when the cow of a careless Irish housewife can be blamed. What about the San Francisco earthquake, or the floods and quakes in China?

A few years ago the TV news showed a Turkish woman renouncing Allah because her grandchild had been killed in a terrible earthquake a few hours before. People find it easier to say that Hitler unnecessarily destroyed the heart of Britain's cities than that God rained bombs on them as He did fire on Sodom. Is it that Sodom deserved judgment while London did not? Or is it that the fires on Sodom may have been natural (volcanic) while the bombs which fell on London were manufactured in Munich or Stuttgart?

A third means of providence is the action of free moral beings, both angels and men, both good and bad. We have already cited certain examples of how God accomplishes His will through the acts of free beings: Joseph and his exile to Egypt through the evil deeds of his brothers, and the rejection of Jesus by the leaders of the Jews, which sent Jesus to Calvary (Acts 2:23).

God's Providence All-inclusive

The Bible is clear that nothing in this entire universe is outside the Creator's providential control. The evidence is varied, but it runs through all parts of the Bible and is overwhelming.

We can only examine here a few of the more comprehensive categories of God's providence with a few selected texts. In most there are dozens of other passages which could be cited.

1. *The physical world.* God's providence rules in this sphere: "Whatever the Lord pleases He does, in heaven and in earth, in the seas and in all deeps. He causes the vapors to ascend from the ends of the earth, who makes lightnings for the rain; who brings forth the wind from His treasuries" (Ps. 135:6-7, NASB); see also Job 37:5, 10; Matt. 5:45; 6:30).

2. *Plant life.* Providence oversees this realm: "The trees of the Lord drink their fill, the cedars of Lebanon which He planted" (Ps. 104:16, NASB). Psalm 104:21, 28 says the lions are fed by God; Matthew 6:26 that He feeds the birds, and Jesus said of sparrows, "not one of them will fall to the ground apart from your Father" (Matt. 10:29, NASB). God also "prepared" the fish featured in Jonah's experiences (Jonah 1:17) as well as the worm (4:7).

3. *Man's social position.* God rules over man's birth, and place in life. David (Ps. 139:16), Jeremiah (Jer. 1:5) and Paul (Gal. 1:15-16) were aware of this. There were many fine families in Israel but the one to provide the new king was prepared by God (1 Sam. 16:1).

4. *Success and failure.* Man's successes and failures are brought about by God, for "not from the east, nor from the west, nor from the desert comes exaltation. But God is the Judge; He puts down one, and exalts another" (Ps. 75:6-7, NASB) and "He hath put down the mighty from their seats, and exalted them of low degree" (Luke 1:52).

5. *Death.* The time and circumstances of a man's death is under God's government. Such was the case with Moses (Deut. 32:48-50) as well as all the adult Israelites who came out of Egypt (Num. 14:29). The same was true of Peter (John 21:18-19). And Job was not mistaken when he said, "In whose hand is the soul of every living thing, and the breath of all mankind" (Job 12:10; see Ps. 104:29).

6. *Guidance and needs.* God supplies the material needs of His people (Matt. 5:45; 6:8, 11, 26; Phil. 4:19) and their spiritual guidance. Paul knew when "Satan hindered" him (1 Thes. 2:18)

and when he was "forbidden by the Holy Ghost" (Acts 16:6). While we may not have the same insights as a prophet or an apostle, we have assurance of His superintendence over our lives.

7. *His care.* God's care for His people is so complete that seeming calamities are blessings in disguise (Phil. 1:12-14; Eph. 3:1).

8. *Grace.* Even the means of God's grace to others (Phil. 1:12-14; Philemon 15) and deliverance from temptations, trials, and persecutions are in God's hands (1 Cor. 10:13; see Dan. 3:17-18).

9. *Trivialities.* Finally, God's providence explains how national events of great moment develop out of seemingly trivial, chance events—a sleepless night (Es. 6:1) or a sad countenance (Neh. 2:1-2). These seeming trivialities are often more decisive than the decisions of judicial and legislative assemblies or executive decisions of national leaders.

Providence and Chance

Does God's providence extend to chance—to what is sometimes called statistical probability? The answer is Yes, with qualification. "The lot is cast into the lap; but the whole disposing thereof is of the Lord" (Prov. 16:33). God is in charge even of card games and roulette wheels.

Christians cannot accept chance as an "undesigned cause" of reality. The regularity and uniformity of the sequences of nature are not assigned to chance in the Bible, even though some scientists base the theory of evolution on chance and explain origins that way. The Bible traces the origin and present integrity of every existing thing to God the Creator.

Occasionally Scripture calls an event *chance,* allowing room for events which happen to people apart from their purposes. Jesus Himself spoke this way (Luke 10:31). It isn't wrong, then, to think of unpurposed human events as occurring by chance. But God has a purpose in every event. *Chance* is simply our name for certain events, and God stoops to use our language.

A paragraph from A. H. Strong gives sensible advice: "Not all chances are of equal importance. The casual meeting of a stranger in the street need not bring God's providence before me, although I know that God arranges it. Yet I can conceive of that meeting as leading to religious conversation and to the stranger's conversion. When we are prepared for them, we shall see many opportunities which are not as unmeaning to us as the gold in the river beds was to the early Indians in California" (*Systematic Theology,* p. 428). Paul calls this "redeeming the time," namely, making use of every opportunity (Eph. 5:16).

Providence and Prayer

Does God's providence leave room for prayer? Jesus said that men ought always to pray (Luke 18:1) and the great Apostle urged us to pray without ceasing (1 Thes. 5:17). Paul, who wrote more about God's decrees and providence than any other writer of Scripture, not only commanded us to pray, but also showed great confidence that God does answer prayer. Thus, the answer to our question is Yes, providence not only leaves room for prayer—it requires it.

By this we mean more than prayer's power to change the one who prays. Daniel was exhausted by his prayers and would not have engaged in prayer unless he anticipated objective results from God (Dan. 7:18; 8:27).

The Christian God is the God of all creation. He has known all along about our prayers. "Before they call, I will answer; and while they are yet speaking, I will hear" (Isa. 65:24); "Then shalt thou call, and the Lord shall answer; thou shalt cry, and He shall say, 'Here I am' " (Isa. 58:9). God's plans include our prayers. God does more than recommend prayer; He commands it and moves our hearts to seek Him in prayer. "The eyes of the Lord are upon the righteous, and His ears are open unto their cry" (Ps. 34:15).

Our prayers must also include God's plans. Once, Jesus asked God to let the cup of Calvary's suffering pass from Him, yet added, "Nevertheless, not My will but Thine be done." He acknowledged that His death for sinners was planned from eternity and that Scripture predicted it.

When we pray we should be sure that the will of God conditions our requests. We cannot command God, nor is strong faith always necessary; Jesus responded favorably to hesitant faith more than once. If, in prayer, we would "ask anything according to His will" (1 John 5:14), we ought also to devote ourselves to diligent Bible study and reflection on Scripture, consulting with Christians wiser than we. All of these are evidences of genuine faith. We must know what God wants and want the same, even if personal loss, suffering, or even death are necessary to bring it to pass. It is not wrong to pray for one's self. The psalmists did and so did our Lord. But effective prayer will certainly focus on God and His plans. Our plans will be adjusted to His.

There can be no *physical* demonstration that God answers prayers. There are moral preconditions which forbid a scientifically controlled situation. God's will is simply not subject to scientific analysis, and His sovereign power cannot be brought to the laboratory. Faith-compelling answers even to saintly prayers are rare. God answered Elijah's prayer for a demonstration of His power for good reasons (1 Kings 18:36-39). But when the Pharisees said to Jesus, "Master, we would see a sign from Thee," Jesus answered, "An evil and adulterous generation seeketh after a sign; and there shall no sign be given to it" (Matt. 12:38-39).

Providence and Christian Effort

Does belief in providence hinder Christian effort? Hardly! Some of the most active evangelists and pastors, philanthropists, and missionaries have had great confidence in God's providence. Both trust *and* effort are God's will for us. We know that God uses means for almost everything He does. And we are His means to accomplish many things.

"You are the only Bible
The careless world will read,
You are the sinner's Gospel,
You are the scoffer's creed."

Prayer without employment of God's means is an insult to Him. If the house catches fire, call on God to put it out, but also call the fire department and get busy with a water bucket.

George Mueller of Bristol, one of the most active Christians who ever lived, had some fine things to say on this subject: "I seek at the beginning to get my heart into such a state that it has no will of its own in regard to a given matter. Nine-tenths of the difficulties are overcome when our hearts are ready to do the Lord's will, whatever it may be. Having done this, I do not leave the result to feeling or simple impression. If I do so, I make myself liable to a great delusion. I seek the will of the Spirit through, or in connection with, the Word of God. The Spirit and the Word must be combined. If I look to the Spirit alone, without the Word, I lay myself open to great delusions also. If the Holy Spirit guides us at all, He will do it according to the Scriptures, and never contrary to them. Next I take into account providential circumstances. These often plainly indicate God's will in connection with His Word and His Spirit. I ask God in prayer to reveal to me His will aright. Thus through prayer to God, the study of His Word, and reflection, I come to a deliberate judgment according to the best of my knowledge and ability, and if my mind is thus at peace, I proceed accordingly." Thus the great founder of Christian orphanages brought prayer, God's will (decrees), and His providence to focus in a marvelously useful life.

Bibliography

Buswell, James O. *Systematic Theology of the Christian Religion,* vol. 1. Grand Rapids: Zondervan, 1962.

Calvin, John. *Calvin: Institutes of the Christian Religion,* vol. 1. Philadelphia: Westminster Press, 1960.

Gerstner, John H. *Reasons for Faith.* New York: Harper and Brothers, 1960.

Henry, Carl F. *Revelation and the Bible.* Grand Rapids: Baker Book House, 1958.

McDonald, H. D. *Theories of Revelation.* London: George Allen and Unwin, Ltd., 1963.

Schneider, Bernard N. *The World of Unseen Spirits.* Winona Lake, Indiana: BMH Books, 1975.

Thiessen, Henry C. *Lectures in Systematic Theology.* Grand Rapids: Eerdmans, 1949.

This reading list, compiled by the author, is not necessarily the recommendation of the publisher.